The WISDOM *of* SUNDAYS

Life-Changing Insights and
Inspirational Conversations

The WISDOM of SUNDAYS

Life-Changing Insights and Inspirational Conversations

OPRAH WINFREY

MACMILLAN

PRODUCED BY

MELCHER MEDIA

First published 2017 by Flatiron Books

First published in the UK 2017 by Macmillan
an imprint of Pan Macmillan
20 New Wharf Road, London N1 9RR
Associated companies throughout the world
www.panmacmillan.com

ISBN 978-1-5098-7411-8

**MELCHER
MEDIA**

Produced by Melcher Media
124 West 13th Street
New York, NY 10011
www.melcher.com

Contributing editorial: Jenna Kostelnik Utley
Cover design: Trina Bentley of Make & Matter
Interior design: Erica Jago
Cover and interior photography: Melissa Gidney Daly

Printed in China

Visit **www.panmacmillan.com** to read more about all our books
and to buy them. You will also find features, author interviews and
news of any author events, and you can sign up for e-newsletters
so that you're always first to hear about our new releases.

I never thought of it that way.

It's a small sentence, but one that I strived to hear and experience
in every interview.

It possesses the spiritual force to *break through* any barrier.
It is weighted with enough depth to *break down* the deepest despair.
It can *break open* the most revelatory "*Aha*" blessings.

It is my great privilege and honor to share these wisdom conversations
I've experienced with some of the great thought leaders of our time.

I offer my endless gratitude to every *Super Soul Sunday* guest whose
spiritual journey and wise words have led me to knowing for sure that
we are all spiritual beings having a human experience.

To the Emmy Award–winning *Super Soul Sunday* team, who helped me
bring my dream to life … including Jenna Kostelnik, who helped craft
all of these teachings into book form.

Thank you, Charles Melcher, Aaron Kenedi, and the Melcher team
for understanding the symbiotic connection between art, nature,
and the human spirit.

Bob Miller, Whitney Frick, and everyone at Flatiron and Macmillan,
thank you for helping shepherd these words into the world.

—*Oprah Winfrey*

CONTENTS

Introduction ... 9

1. AWAKENING ... 13

2. INTENTION ... 45

3. MINDFULNESS ... 61

4. SPIRITUAL GPS ... 79

5. EGO ... 97

6. FORGIVENESS ... 111

7. BROKEN OPEN ... 125

8. GRACE AND GRATITUDE ... 151

9. FULFILLMENT ... 173

10. LOVE AND CONNECTION ... 199

Epilogue ... 221

Contributors ... 227

Credits and Acknowledgments ... 240

All of us are seeking the same thing. We share the desire to fulfill the highest, truest expression of ourselves as human beings.

—*Oprah*

INTRODUCTION

I believe part of my calling on Earth is to help people connect to ideas that expand their vision of who they *really* are and all they can be.

That's why I created *Super Soul Sunday*. After filming more than two hundred hours of heart-expanding interviews, I began to envision a truly transcendent book—with words you can hold in your hand, be inspired by, and carry with you forever.

The photos also hold deep meaning for me. Many of the images you'll see were taken at my home in Santa Barbara, where I feel the presence of God, and the connection to *All* that is greater than myself, most deeply. Morning walks with my dogs represent a form of prayer for me, taking time to delight in the glory of nature that surrounds me. Baby tears grass laced between a stone path, fallen

acorns, a bird's nest, these photos represent to me both the majestic abundance of our shared world and the unseen details we often miss in our lives. Like spirituality itself, the simplest things, when appreciated with reverence, take on an entirely new meaning. Suddenly that single blade of grass has gone from ordinary to poignant to explicit and finally miraculous in its beauty.

As you read *The Wisdom of Sundays*, my prayer is that you will uncover the little spaces in your own life, find comfort in them, gain insight to their meaning, and see the way forward to an extraordinary new existence.

Within these pages, I've collected some of the most powerful spiritual lessons, sparks of brilliance, and *aha* moments from *Super Soul Sunday* that continue to resonate with me today.

What I know for sure is the most valuable gift you can give yourself is the time to nurture the unique spirit that is you. Your life, just like mine, is unfolding according to your own truth. No one has been through what you have been through, not in the way that you've experienced it. And yet, all pain is the same. Our sadness and sorrows, joys and triumphs bind us in the common thread of humanity. The sooner we realize the connection, the more elevated life becomes.

What you will learn from these spiritual teachers is that with every decision, you are claiming the essence of the phenomenon that is your life.

The great American mythologist, author, and philosopher Joseph Campbell once said, *"The privilege of a lifetime is being who you are."*

I believe your true purpose here on Earth is to align yourself with the great spiritual force, your divine inner compass, already at work in your life.

I hope that *The Wisdom of Sundays* will illuminate your path to becoming all that you were meant to be.

Embrace and enjoy the journey!

—*Oprah*

Spirituality for me is recognizing that I am connected to the energy of all creation, that I am a part of it and it is always a part of me.

—Oprah

CHAPTER ONE

AWAKENING

Years ago, I invited renowned spiritual teacher Caroline Myss to be a guest on *The Oprah Winfrey Show*.

I had just been introduced to Caroline's groundbreaking work on healing and intuition and was so excited about what I had learned that I couldn't wait to share it with the audience. I hoped they might experience the same spiritual awakening.

Unfortunately, that's not what happened.

For the first few minutes, Caroline and I were totally engrossed in our conversation about spirituality and nurturing the soul. But eventually we reached a point where I noticed that the people in the audience were looking at us like we were speaking a foreign language. I stopped the taping and asked if they understood what Caroline and I were talking about. One woman bravely stood up and said, "No, we really don't. What do you mean by spirit? Are you talking about Jesus?"

"No," I said. "We're talking about you."

The woman went on to say that she thought the word *spirit* meant something outside of herself, similar to how she viewed religion.

This was an epiphany for me. I realized concepts like spirituality and the soul were unfamiliar ones for many people at that time.

We have come a long way since then, but I'm forever grateful to that woman for speaking up. It is a wonderful reminder that every single person is at a different stage of their own spiritual evolution. And no path is the same.

We eventually resumed taping, and I asked Caroline to explain her definition of the word *spirit*. And now, years later, in most *Super Soul Sunday* conversations, I ask that same question: What does spirituality mean to you?

The message running through every lesson in this chapter is that each one of us has been blessed with an individual spiritual essence.

As you begin to establish a deeper connection to that innate presence within you, certain passages from *The Wisdom of Sundays* might feel like a direct spark to your heart—a big lightning bolt, or a little shiver that shouts, "Yes!"

I know this, because I experienced it, too! When something clicks so profoundly, it feels like a light bulb illuminating the truth. As these great spiritual teachers taught me, this is your awakening. It's resonating because it's spirit recognizing spirit.

That is the ultimate *aha* moment.

—*Oprah*

Your spirit is the part of you
that is seeking meaning and
purpose. That's one way someone
can relate to that. Another way
to understand spirit is that it's
the part of you that is drawn
to hope, that will not give in to
despair. The part of you that has
to believe in goodness; that has
to believe in something more.

—*Caroline Myss*

GARY ZUKAV

I'm talking about an expansion of your perception beyond the five senses, beyond what you can see and taste and touch and hear and smell. As people become multisensory, they begin to become aware. Millions of us are acquiring that sense that life has a meaning, that I have a purpose, that I am more than this mind and body. I'm more than molecules and dendrites and neurons and enzymes.

I have a part of me that is immortal. Multisensory perception does not make us more kind or patient or caring or less angry. It makes us more aware. And when you get that sense, the spiritual work begins.

ECKHART TOLLE

ECKHART TOLLE: The real truths of life are never entirely new to you because there is a level deep down within you where you already know all the things, all those spiritual truths that you read or hear and then recognize them. Ultimately, it's not new information.

OPRAH: *It's a resonation. It's resonating with what is somehow buried or suppressed.*

ECKHART: Yes.

OPRAH: *Your consciousness is recognizing the consciousness of whatever that message is.*

ECKHART: Yes. And that's an awakening. And that knowing in you awakens and then it grows. It comes to the surface more. And the more it grows, the more open you are to hearing spiritual truths. And then you begin to live it in your life.

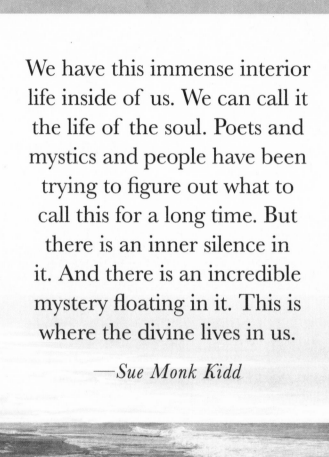

We have this immense interior life inside of us. We can call it the life of the soul. Poets and mystics and people have been trying to figure out what to call this for a long time. But there is an inner silence in it. And there is an incredible mystery floating in it. This is where the divine lives in us.

—*Sue Monk Kidd*

DEEPAK CHOPRA

I want to give you just a very brief, and very quick, understanding of these different areas of our life that we call the body, the mind, the soul. Your body is mostly carbon, hydrogen, oxygen, and nitrogen. You have stardust that was once circulating in that body. There are at least a million atoms in your body. In just the last three weeks, a quadrillion atoms have gone through your body that have gone through the body of every other living species on this planet. We experience our body as this three-dimensional structure in space and time.

We know where the mind is. We experience it as our thoughts, our feelings, our emotions, our ideas. But where is the soul? Between every thought, we have a little space. That still presence that you feel, that's your soul. It was there when you were a baby. It was there when you were a teenager. It's there now. It will be there tomorrow. And if you get really in touch with it, if you become familiar with this center of awareness that you really are, you will see it's your ticket to freedom.

MICHAEL BERNARD BECKWITH

Everyone is spiritual whether they know it or not. When I consider what it means to be spiritual, I consider the fact that individuals are waking up to a dimension of their being or their soul. It is the most real part of us. When one begins to really feel into the spiritual dimension of their being, they bump into love. They bump into compassion. They bump into beauty. They bump into real peace and real joy. And that begins to be where they live their life from, real, authentic beings that have a tremendous amount of meaning in their life.

JACK KORNFIELD

JACK KORNFIELD: To live an awakened life is to be here in the reality of the present, in the now, which is all we have. And to recognize that thoughts about the future are thoughts. You can use them, but you don't have to believe them, because half the time they don't come true. And thoughts about the past are gone. The past, you can learn from.

To be awake is to live here so that when you are with the person you love, you're really present, or with your dog, or with the work that you're devoting yourself to, or your creative life. Or whether you listen to your heart and realize that you are caught in fear and confusion. The poet Hafiz says, *"Fear is the cheapest room in the house. I'd like to see you in better living conditions."*

So, to live awake is to sense that the fear or contraction or confusion that we have is not the end of the story. We have a capacity for freedom and dignity, no matter what.

OPRAH: *With all that you know, what is it you would most want to offer about beginning to live a more awakened life?*

JACK: Okay, the first would be to say that it's worth it to stop and quiet yourself. Do whatever you need. If it's getting up earlier in the morning, or staying up a little bit later, or building in that walk, or even waiting a few seconds and taking a breath before you press the Send button on the e-mail or the tweet, and quieting yourself and saying, "What's my best intention?" Because if you listen to your heart and ask, "What's my best intention?" it will answer. There's a kind of conversation you can have if you quiet yourself. So the first thing is to look for moments in the day and times that you can build in to come back with respect and listen to yourself. And the people who find their way to quiet themselves, they find their own art, just as they learn how to cook. Just as they learn how to drive. They can learn an inner art—and find a practice that works for them. The second wish is compassion and forgiveness.

OPRAH: *You can't live without it.*

JACK: Without forgiveness, the world is lost. It's like those two prisoners of war that met years later, and one said to the other, "Have you forgiven your captors yet?" And the second one said, "No, I never will." And then the first one said, "Well, then, they still have you in prison, don't they?" So there's some way in which you can free yourself from the past through forgiveness, and it means forgiveness for yourself, for all the foolishness and ways that you've been caught that you didn't know.

OPRAH: *And people do it in ways, in myriads of ways, that they don't even know.*

JACK: And the beautiful truth is that you can let go.

OPRAH: *You can.*

JACK: It is possible for you to let go, and there's a very simple practice of forgiveness, of looking into the heart, in which you hold yourself with forgiveness and you repeat it over and over in these very, very simple ways. At first, it doesn't feel like it works at all. It's sort of like water on a stone. "I'll never forgive that person. I'll never forgive myself." And then at some point, you realize they could be on vacation in the Bahamas right now, having a great time,

and you're there resenting, and who's suffering?

We've all been foolish at times, and instead of treating ourselves with a lack of forgiveness for ourselves or for others, we can see it, hold it with compassion, forgiveness, and say, "Now this is the third wish, that you could live with joy and well-being. And that this is your birthright. The Buddhist teachings begin with this kind of exhortation: Do not forget your original wholeness, your original goodness and beauty, and turn yourself toward what is good. Turn your heart toward what is good by cultivating forgiveness and compassion and mindful presence. See the good in one another. Nelson Mandela said, "It never hurts to see the good in someone. They often act the better because of it."

OPRAH: *That's beautiful.*

JACK: If you're a schoolteacher and you see the beauty in those kids, they love you as a teacher, and it gets reflected, and they feel, "I'm gonna do my best because this teacher sees me and gets me." And so you can choose. You can actually turn toward your innate goodness.

OPRAH: *Isn't that what everybody wants? I mean, in all of my talks and understandings over the years, doing thousands and thousands of shows, I came away with the understanding that the thread that runs through all of our human experience is that we all want to be validated. We all want to be seen, we all want to know that we matter. And the most you can ever do for somebody is to show up and allow them to know that they have been seen and heard by you.*

JACK: That's music to my ears. When somebody says, "I'd like a little attention," it's not a little thing they're asking. I like to think of it as loving awareness—that when you give someone attention, it's somehow a marrying of your presence with their presence and also within that presence, there's love. That you really see the beauty that's behind the eyes of that person.

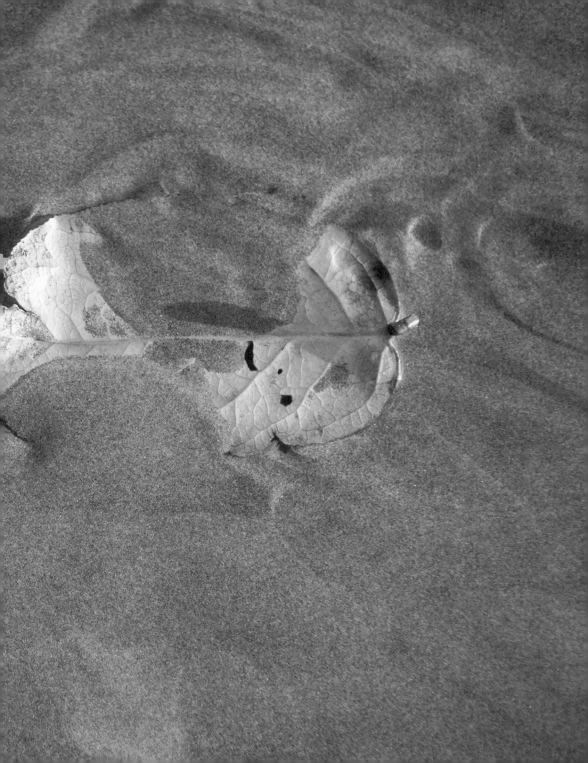

RAM DASS

OPRAH: *You had a transformational moment with a guru you met in India?*

RAM DASS: We drove toward the foothills of the Himalayas and stopped at a roadside temple. Here's the scene—a man with a blanket, he's seated on a table, and about twenty people are around him, and he's talking.

OPRAH: *Sitting at his feet?*

RAM DASS: Sitting at his feet, white gowns and all. So I stood back because I didn't want to get involved.

OPRAH: *In any of that business.*

RAM DASS: Yeah. Well, he pointed at me. He was speaking Hindu. And he said, "You were out under the stars last night, and you were thinking about your mother." He said, "Your mother died." And I said, "Yes." Now how did he know that? He said, "Spleen," which is the name of the organ that killed my mother.

OPRAH: *That's when you went, "Whoa!"*

RAM DASS: Yeah.

OPRAH: *"Who is this guy?"*

RAM DASS: Yeah, "Who is that?" How did he know? I didn't tell anybody. That was a miracle in a way. He was reading my mind. And I said, "If he knows that, he'll know, ooh, ooh, ooh."

OPRAH: *If he knows that, then he knows me. He knows all my secrets.*

RAM DASS: And I looked up at him, and he was looking at me with unconditional love, unconditional love. He was loving me totally. It had never happened before. People love you because you're a good boy, you're a good friend. And he was loving me, all of me, all the stuff of me that I never wanted anybody to know.

OPRAH: *Right, that's what everybody fears, "If you really knew me." If you really knew me, you wouldn't really love me.*

RAM DASS: Exactly. And this, he knew me and he loved me. And I found myself saying, "Home again."

OPRAH: *How do you explain that when you sat in front of the Maharaji, you not only felt love, but became love, and loved people, too?*

RAM DASS: He mirrored my soul. And made me identify with my soul and not my ego. This was who I thought I was and who I was really. And he said, "I want you to love everybody."

OPRAH: *So you came back to spread the love, the message of love.*

RAM DASS: Yes.

ELIZABETH LESSER

ELIZABETH LESSER: Spirituality is an instinct. You know we have our instincts to eat and to sleep, and to work and survive, and thrive that way. But we also have a spiritual instinct. It's really inside every person. That's why religions were formed, to respond to that instinct, to know that life has meaning, to know that we are connected to everything, and to have that child-like sense of wonder that we were put here to enjoy the gift of life.

OPRAH: *Yes. Spirituality is that yearning for something more, that desire that is seeking something higher than your mind and your body.*

ROB BELL

ROB BELL: To me, the only kind of faith worth having is faith that can celebrate the good and the true and the beautiful wherever you find it. It's a big, buoyant, expansive embrace of everything, everywhere you find it.

OPRAH: *You know, my definition of God is the All. The All in the All, through the All, above the All …*

ROB: That's a good one.

OPRAH: *You basically say the same thing. "I understand God to be the"—these are your words—"the energy, the glue, the force, the life, the power, the source of all we know to be. The depth, the fullness, vitality of life from the highest of the highs to the lowest of the lows. And everything in between." I think that's the All.*

ROB: Yes, exactly, first and foremost, to all the really smart, studied people who have been to a TED conference and have iPhones, it's not crazy to acknowledge that there's a God. It may actually be the most rational move. It's simply to say, "I come to the end of my own logical powers and acknowledge there's too much that's beyond what we can sort through using these little brains that we have." And for three hundred years, the water we've been swimming in, that we've been handed by the enlightenment tradition, which has brought us medicines and hospitals and all sorts of wonderful things, has also brought us, ultimately, something you cannot explain. And yet we're fascinated as humans. We're wired for the mysterious. We love it. We're drawn to it. You can't stifle it.

OPRAH: *So you're saying just open to that.*

ROB: It's okay to be open.

OPRAH: *What you're suggesting is that we open ourselves up to a broader definition of God. And your core spiritual beliefs are, number one, that God is with us. Number two, that God is for us. Number three, that God is ahead of us. If we look for it, we can experience the life, the power, the source of all we know to be in every moment.*

ROB: For many people in the modern world, God is somewhere else, generally with a long beard on a cloud. And He was quite grumpy until Jesus came.

OPRAH: *Absolutely. And when I was a kid, my version was that He was on a cloud, long beard, white robes, and had a big, black book.*

ROB: And when He opened it, it was like *boom.* And so this God is somewhere else and then from time to time, people say, "Then God showed up." Only I don't think God shows up. I think we show up for God.

OPRAH: *Oh, I do, too. High-five that.*

ROB: So what's fascinating is the ancient Hebrews have this word *ruach,* which is the life force that surges through all things. And the word in the very beginning of Genesis 1? The spirit hovering, but for many people in our world, spirit is that which is less real. You know what I mean? Oh, it's spiritual, meaning this other realm. And then there's awe! We've all experienced that … moment of "awe." I simply want to give the name God to that. So the person who says, "Oh, I don't know if I believe in God," but deep down, in the hospital when your kid was born? Well, what else was that? What I'm trying to do in the book is simply move a person's conception from somewhere out here, optional, to the very thing we're all plugged into.

OPRAH: *That we're experiencing the presence of in every single day.*

ROB: All the time. All around us. And so then, as a human, the art of it then is being awake and open and aware and sensitive to this presence. Right here and now, in suffering and in joy. That's what I mean by "with us."

LLEWELLYN VAUGHAN-LEE

LLEWELLYN VAUGHAN-LEE: People come into this world and they forget their divine nature. They become caught in what the Chinese call the "10,000 things" of life.

OPRAH: *I would say the world is caught in that right now.*

LLEWELLYN: Yes, very sadly, the world is caught. And then there comes this moment in their life when something wakes them up. It's a very magical moment. I'll tell you a story. Once, I was traveling to New York on an airplane and I went to use the bathroom, and there was a line. I saw that the flight attendant was reading a book about dreams that I happened to know. And I said, "Oh, interesting book." She started to tell me her story, and said she had just been to a workshop. And then she said, "I suddenly discovered there's more to life than getting stuff." I could see this light in her eyes. She had woken up. She'd realized there is something within her. It wasn't just about material accumulation. It was this magical moment when something awakens within the heart of the human being.

OPRAH: *Unfortunately, for so many people I've interviewed, that moment happens when tragedy strikes.*

LLEWELLYN: That's right.

OPRAH: *And a lot of people use that experience for their own awakening. But you believe you don't have to go through a terrible time.*

LLEWELLYN: It is a gift. It's always a gift, that moment, however it comes. The Sufis talk about the homesickness of the soul. Something calls to you, and you take respect and value that moment. And then begin the journey to God.

OPRAH: *And what does the journey to God feel like?*

LLEWELLYN: It can be an experience of oneness; you get taken to the oneness that is all around you, that is part of life. It can be an experience of love. You get drawn into this love. You begin to lose yourself in love. And suddenly there is no longer you, there is just love.

We're talking about the God who is life. Who is all of energy. Who is the seed of everything that ever existed. Who burst into the Universe with everything that we'll ever see and ever be able to be. Now, if that God is the ultimate, primary seed of all life, that's my seed, as well as His seed. And you cannot have a consciousness of God unless you have a consciousness of life in all of its forms.

—*Sister Joan Chittister*

THOMAS MOORE

THOMAS MOORE: I think religion is something that is quite natural. It's something that we do as human beings. So we face mysteries. Illness is a great mystery. Death is a mystery. Marriage is a mystery. All these things. And I don't think we can deal with all this rationally, so we need something. On the other hand, we've made a turn somewhere—I think largely because of changes in our culture—and the old forms don't work as well anymore. They work for some people, but even then, you have to reinvigorate them.

OPRAH: *So creating a religion of your own, some people call this a smorgasbord religion. Taking a little bit from this and a little bit from that. And where is the order? Where is the discipline? Where is the one true God in all of that? I think when we speak of creating a religion of one's own, people think that also means creating a God of one's own.*

THOMAS: Well, I'll put it this way. When I was studying theology and religion all those years as a monk,

I learned that God is unknowable and infinite. Unknowable and infinite, that's what I was always taught.

OPRAH: *Oh, I love that.*

THOMAS: So if you make God, then, into a sort of human version, a human being kind of God, or you anthropomorphize as they say, or make Him human, like a human being, you've diminished the whole—you don't have a God anymore. You could have a superhuman being, but you don't have a God. You don't have a real sense of the divine.

OPRAH: *But what about the passages in the Bible and other religious books that say we are created in His image?*

THOMAS: Well, we are. I think that we have within us, if we go deep enough inside ourselves, we touch on the infinite. We really do.

OPRAH: *I think you can't emphasize that enough. Because I think most people never go deep enough to understand what that means, that we are in His image because people are thinking that it's the physical thing. And it is not.*

THOMAS: No. Here's a big issue, I think. The world we live in tends to see everything mechanistically or physically alone. They don't understand that there is some invisible dimension to our experience. To everything. Even to nature. And so we tend to reduce things too much.

OPRAH: *We reduce things to what we can see.*

THOMAS: What we can see and touch.

OPRAH: *And define things, even our God, by what we can see. By what we can see and touch.*

ELIZABETH GILBERT

Sartre said, "Exits are everywhere." But I feel like entrances are everywhere. And I think that the world would be an even more cruel place than it already is, if the only people who are allowed to go on spiritual journeys were people who could afford a plane ticket to India, you know? Because we all know that people find access to God through those thin places in the Universe and the thin places in their lives where they come very close to the divine, in all sorts of situations. You know, in prison, in their house, in the middle of the night, in the middle of a bad marriage, in the middle of a traffic jam. It's always there. There's an entrance that you can slide through. But I really do feel like the one non-negotiable thing that you need is to be able to find a tiny little corner of your life, of your day of stillness, where you can begin to ask yourself those burning essential questions of your life. Who am I? Where did I come from? Where am I going? What am I here for? And for that you need to find a sacred moment of silence to begin to look for that journey. And that's available to everybody.

Pastor JOHN GRAY

PASTOR JOHN GRAY: I'm a nature guy, even though I live in a big city. You put me next to a creek, put me next to a tree, let me see the birds fly through the air, I feel God. I used to feel God in thunderstorms.

OPRAH: *Really?*

JOHN: Oh, absolutely. In our two-bedroom apartment in Cincinnati, we had no air conditioners. We had a fence behind my window. At nine and ten years old, I'd walk out through our little clearing into the stars, and I would tell God what I wanted to do. I told Him I wanted to be a husband. I told Him if I ever fail Him, please don't leave me. I wanted Him to be proud of me. I wanted Him to use my life to do something great. And then when we'd have those big Midwest thunderstorms in the middle of summer and spring, I'd run to the front porch and I'd sit out there because just feeling the rain on my feet made me feel like God

was talking to me, especially when I would hear the thunder and see the lightning. My mom would say, "Come off the porch. The lightning will get you." I said, "My dad is in charge of that. I'm talking to Him right now." And she would allow me to sit out there. And that's the way I connected to God. That's how He speaks to me. For some reason, storms give me peace. Because I know He's in charge of it. So in the same way He's in charge of the natural storms, He's in charge of my spiritual storms. My emotional storms. The human condition. When I'm broken, when I want to give up, I know He's there.

OPRAH: *What would you say to some-one who wants some of that? Who wants to feel that kind of connection and passion and relationship? I know there are some people who will be saying the God you're talking about is not in my church.*

JOHN: Right. That God is a God I encounter away from the hour-and-a-half service on Sunday.

OPRAH: *Aha.*

JOHN: That's the God I talk to at two in the morning. That's the one where I'm crying tears, trying to figure out and believing that there was still purpose.

OPRAH: *Is every prayer heard?*

JOHN: Yes. Every prayer is not answered the way you may want it, but they are all heard. I believe that. How could the one who created us ignore us? Some people will say, "Well, He hasn't answered my prayer." People miss that all prayers are heard. But sometimes the answer is no. And so for me, I've had to grow and say, Does my worship or my exuberance for God change? Because sometimes the answer is no. And where I'm learning how to mature is that whether I get the yes or the no, I'm still content in all things.

MICHAEL SINGER

MICHAEL SINGER: There's something we listen to on a regular basis. The problem is we think it's us. So, for example, you look at a vase and it says, "That's a very interesting shape, but I don't really like the color that much. It reminds me of my grandmother's vase." And all of a sudden, we have somebody narrating and talking inside our head. That is not you, right?

OPRAH: *Right, those are all your thoughts about the vase.*

MICHAEL: And more and more, as I watched that, I realized it never shuts up, that it talks about everything, it judges everything, it thinks about everything.

OPRAH: *Right. And you became aware of the thoughts running through your head during a lull in conversation with a friend, right? You say you realized that incessant voice that expresses worries and doubts and anxieties was not really you, but you were the observer of the voice. Realizing that inner dialogue was an expression of the psyche, not the soul, was the beginning of your awakening?*

MICHAEL: Yes, that was the beginning of my path.

OPRAH: *So what actually happened in that moment now that you can describe? Eckhart Tolle has said that the awareness, the voice, the awareness of the thoughts, or the awareness of the voice inside your head, is where consciousness resides, and that is who we really are. So that's what you came to?*

MICHAEL: Yes.

OPRAH: *That was your open door to the path to understanding yourself as a spiritual being inside a physical human body.*

MICHAEL: With a mind. That's correct.

OPRAH: *And isn't this the most important thing ever…*

MICHAEL: Period. It's the most important thing.

OPRAH: *The road to the spiritual path is to understand that you are a spiritual being And the way to understand that you are a spiritual being is to know that you are not all of those thoughts.*

MICHAEL: Yes. Because so far, we can't say what you are, because that's a thought, right? And you are there watching these thoughts. Sometimes people say to me, "But which of those are me?" None of them are you. You're the one who's watching.

OPRAH: *Okay, so I got this really clearly when I was in India and there was a yogi who was leading me in meditation. It was just the two of us, and he said, "Close your eyes, and now I'm going to name different objects." One of the objects was a red triangle and one was the moon and one was a white picket fence. And he said, "Hold on to the objects in your mind, and then when I name the next object, let it go." What I realized, in that conscious moment, was that's what is happening all the time. Red triangles and picket fences and chairs and thoughts about everything are coming in. "I'm not good enough, I lost my job, I can't believe he left me, I can't believe my kids did that." They're thoughts.*

MICHAEL: They're thoughts. They are not you.

OPRAH: *They are not you. So how do we begin to separate ourselves from the thoughts? That's the question.*

MICHAEL: Right, and that's the key. What I love is that you said that really is the beginning of spirituality.

OPRAH: *It is!*

MICHAEL: Because to separate what you're not from what you are, if you don't do that, you're going to stay lost. The self is spiritual. The one who's watching is the gateway to spirituality. So if you continue to just get involved in the mind, in the thoughts in the mind, this true spiritual path doesn't take place.

*The number one principle
that rules my life is
intention. Thought by
thought, choice by choice,
we are cocreating our
lives based on the energy
of our intention.*

—Oprah

CHAPTER TWO

INTENTION

I can say with certainty that had I not read Gary Zukav's book *The Seat of the Soul,* there would be no *Super Soul Sunday.*

There would be no OWN, and *The Oprah Winfrey Show* would probably not have been on the air for twenty-five years (it would have ended sooner). Anyone who knows me knows the principle of intention that I learned from Gary changed the way I approach everything. In fact, I talk about the importance of intention so much that people often recite my own words back to me! Just hearing, "Intention rules every outcome," makes me want to stand up and cheer.

The lesson I learned from my conversations with Gary and the other spiritual teachers in this chapter may sound simple, but it is the truth behind all relationships: The energy we put out in the world is the energy we get back. So if you want more love in your life, set your intention to be more loving. If you seek kindness, focus your energy on empathy and compassion. Conversely, if you wonder why there are so many angry people in your life, look no further than the resentment you hold in your own heart.

Anyone who's on the path of a spiritual awakening needs to know that it's sometimes difficult. It's challenging when you declare, "I want to grow, I want to be better than I've known myself to be." But I don't see the opportunity to craft our own lives as a burden. I see it as one of the gifts of being alive.

For so many years, I suffered from what I call a "disease to please." I worried that if I ever said *no* to something, people were going to think I wasn't nice, or they might think I was selfish and ask, "Why wouldn't she do that for me?" The power of intention cured me of that. I stopped listening to that little voice in my head that was trying to convince me of what other people thought. I made the shift to listen to the truth of who I really was, telling me what I really wanted.

This shift can happen for you, too. Before you agree to do anything that might add even the smallest amount of stress to your life, ask yourself, *What is my truest intention?* Give yourself time to let the answer resound within you. When the intention is right and the answer is *yes,* I guarantee, your entire body will feel it.

—*Oprah*

GARY ZUKAV

GARY ZUKAV: So we were talking about intention. Let's start there.

OPRAH: *Yes, yes, let's start with intention, yes.*

GARY: An intention is the quality of consciousness that you bring to a deed or words. It's an energy. It's your reason for speaking. It's your motivation that creates consequences. For example, when someone says, "I want a bigger home," it could be because they want to impress the neighbors, or it could be because they've adopted four children and they want to give the kids more space. So it's the why beneath the why.

OPRAH: *The why beneath the why.*

GARY: You might say the first intention like, "I want to get another job, so I can have more money." This could be called an *outention*. Because it's what you really want to do to change things and the world. Your intention is the bedrock, this is that real intention: "I want to support my wife, she needs some support right now. I want to send my children to college, I want to have room for my newly adopted children."

OPRAH: *And what you're saying here is that the consciousness or energy behind the motivation is going to determine the effect that occurs.*

GARY: Precisely.

Pastor JOEL OSTEEN

OPRAH: *I heard a sermon that you preached on the power of "I am." And that sermon literally changed how I spoke power into my own life. I was shooting* The Butler. *I had heard that sermon. I was exhausted. We'd been shooting and shooting and shooting And your voice came into my head—that whatever follows "I am" will determine what your experience will be. And so I literally thought, I'm going to try that because I'm exhausted. And I started saying, "I am getting my second wind. I am going to feel so much better by midnight, I'm going to want to shoot all night." And I'm telling you, I started to feel differently. And I couldn't believe that it happened so quickly.*

PASTOR JOEL OSTEEN: It's an incredible principle, I don't think we realize that what follows "I am," we're inviting into our life. You know, you say, "I am tired," "I am frustrated," "I am lonely," you've invited that in. So the principle is to turn it around and invite what you want into your life.

OPRAH: *So whatever follows "I am" will eventually find you.*

JOEL: Yeah. I think a lot of times you're going to say how you feel.

I am lonely. I am tired. There's a balance to it. I don't think you're denying the facts. Otherwise, I'm just hiding my head in the sand. It's not so much that, it's just not magnifying the negative. I talk about "I am the masterpiece," "I am fearfully and wonderfully made," "I am strong," "I am talented." That is speaking more to the core of what God put in each one of us. He has equipped us, he has empowered us. We have what we need to fulfill our destiny. But I do think that we have to bring it out. And you can't bring it out being against yourself. And I think that is what keeps us from our destiny.

OPRAH: *So we've heard that phrase, "Speaking truth to power." It feels like when you understand that whatever follows "I am" is going to eventually find you, that if you start speaking all the positive aspects of yourself—"I am secure," "I am valuable," "I am approved," "I am determined," "I am generous"—when you start allowing what you want to be your truth, you begin to speak truth, the truth of "I am" to the power of what can be.*

TONY ROBBINS

OPRAH: *What is the number-one rule you would offer someone to becoming their most authentic self? Because that's really what we're all looking for. How do I just be more of me?*

TONY ROBBINS: I think it's allowing yourself to be spontaneous instead of responding to how you think you're supposed to be. We've all developed an identity, a sense of who we think we are and who we're not. You define yourself not only by who you think you are but also by who you're not. And those definitions were usually made ten, twenty, thirty, forty years ago. And we rarely upgrade them unless we have an abrupt experience that makes us reevaluate our lives. So to consciously decide, "Who am I today? What do I stand for? What am I here for? What am I here to give? What am I here to learn? What am I here to grow? What am I here to enjoy?" And then to spontaneously try things. Because I think the most important decision is saying, "I'm gonna enjoy this moment right now. It's the only thing I have that's real. And life's too short to suffer." And if I just keep doing that with each moment, things unfold in a way that's, as you know, beyond magnificent. And it's easy to teach, harder to apply, but it's a discipline. And if you do it, and you start measuring it moment to moment, you will get addicted. It will be a positive addiction because the liberation is beyond what you can describe with words. You have to experience it.

Your vision is for you. And there will be many times when other people can't see your vision. That's all right because if God gave you the vision, God will give you the provision. God is not going to bring your provision through your sister's vision. It's going to come to you, for you, through you, as soon as you eliminate the deficiencies.

—*Iyanla Vanzant*

DAVID BROOKS

OPRAH: *I love how you say we should rank our loves in highs and lows. Tell me what that does.*

DAVID BROOKS: That's a concept from the great theologian Augustine. And he asked the question, what is sin? When we use the word *sin* now, we only use the word in the context of fattening desserts. But in traditional morality, it's the sense that we have something broken. And I don't like the word *sin* when it's meant to suggest we're dark and depraved inside. But Augustine had a beautiful formula. He said, "We sin when we have our loves out of order." And what he meant by that—

OPRAH: *Oh, this is good. "We sin when we have our loves out of order." Yes.*

DAVID: So we all love a lot of things. We love family. We love money. We love a little affection. Status. Truth. And we all know that some loves are higher. We know that our love of family is higher than our love of money. Or our love of truth should be higher than our love of money. And if we're lying to get money, we're putting our loves out of order. And so sometimes just by our nature, we get them out of order. So, for example, if a friend tells you a secret, and you blab it at a dinner party, you're putting your love of popularity above your love of friendship. And we know that's wrong. That's the wrong order. And so it's useful to sit down and say, "What do I love? What are the things I really love? And in what order do I love them? Am I spending time on my highest love? Or am I spending time on a lower love?"

BRENÉ BROWN

OPRAH: *What does it mean to dare greatly?*

BRENÉ BROWN: To me, it means the courage to be vulnerable. It means to show up and be seen. To ask for what you need. To talk about how you're feeling. To have the hard conversations. We asked people in the research, "What is vulnerability to you?"

OPRAH: *Most people think vulnerability is weakness.*

BRENÉ: Right.

OPRAH: *And you know what? After reading* Daring Greatly, *what I realized, first of all, is I live in the space of vulnerability. And what has made me so successful is my vulnerability with the audience.*

BRENÉ: For sure.

OPRAH: *And I think that vulnerability is the cornerstone of confidence. Because you have to allow yourself to take the risk to be open, to live as a wholehearted person. When you can do that, you recognize that you're really just like everybody else, and that gives you the confidence to be yourself, which is all you really need in life, to be more of yourself.*

BRENÉ: That's it. And you can't get to courage without walking through vulnerability, period.

SUE MONK KIDD

I marched into the kitchen, where my husband was getting our two toddlers to eat their cereal, and made my big annunciation, I'm going to be a writer. And I was getting in touch with that creative desire inside of me. I was going to write. Because that had been an innate desire in me as a child. You know, you find this little light in yourself, and then of course you lose it and you have to refind it. I mean, that's part of finding our place of belonging.

My husband said, "Ooh, that's great," you know, and continued to get the children to eat their cereal. And that was it.

I didn't know anything about writing. I kept a journal from time to time. That was something that I had done as a child. When I was a little girl, I used to write little stories and newspapers and all kinds of things. But until I was thirty, I really had not pursued it. I had walked away from it.

But when we make that kind of statement, it's an annunciation to ourselves, to the powers that be, to the divine, *This is my intention.* So I think it helps to say our intention out loud. And then the moment I said it, of course, I thought, *What do I know about this?* It is a great absurdity. But everybody needs a great absurdity. At least one of them, right?

DEVON FRANKLIN

OPRAH: *One of the things that you say that really struck me is that if we look at our life as a movie and God as the director of our movie, then we use our faith to help propel us forward in trusting in the director, correct?*

DEVON FRANKLIN: Yes. Absolutely. Because what I realized is that sometimes we, in the most difficult times in our story, we begin to lose faith.

OPRAH: *And start to think we're in control of things. But all it takes is one wrong turn and we quickly remember that's just not true. Here is what I love. You say: "The truth is, you and I are in control of only two things: how we prepare for what might happen, and how we respond to what just happened. The moment when things actually do happen belongs to God."*

DEVON: Amen.

OPRAH: *Brilliant. Brilliant.*

DEVON: It's true. Because what happens is, the moments when things happen in our life, we don't control. In a moment, life can change for the better or what in the moment may seem for the worse. So our job is to prepare.

OPRAH: *Prepare for only two things.*

DEVON: That's right.

OPRAH: *Prepare for what might happen. And then how we respond to what has happened.*

DEVON: That's right. Because so many times what keeps us in that valley of depression, what keeps us in that valley of frustration, is our response to a moment and not recognizing that it is exactly that. It's a moment. It's one scene of your movie. And what makes a great movie are scenes that are put together of great conflict.

OPRAH: *Okay. You also say: "The key is remembering your story. The spiritual journey parallels the steps involved in bringing a movie from the initial idea to theatrical release."*

DEVON: Yes.

OPRAH: *So you start with the kernel of an idea, a process known as development and production. And development begins when you have the first vision of what you can be, correct?*

DEVON: Exactly. You can't write a movie unless you know what the movie is supposed to be about. That's what development is. Sometimes we get so frustrated in our lives, but we have to go back and say, "Wait a minute. Do I understand what the big idea of my life is supposed to be?" If my life is a story, then I have to know the point of my story. And sometimes what happens when we start developing a movie, the producers may have one vision of what the movie is supposed to be and the studio has another version and then the movie becomes nothing because there's no clarity. So with our life, we have to have clarity of what we're supposed to do. What do we believe we're called to do in this life? And then that way it gives our whole development process more shape.

OPRAH: *I am getting goose bumps right now. You know why?*

DEVON: Why?

OPRAH: *Because I know that the way that landed with me and the way I heard it—and that anybody who's hearing you also can hear it—I can feel the kernel of, "If you are not in control of the development of your life, or aware that your life needs developing, and you are just waking up every morning, going to a job, going through the motions, getting your paycheck, then really it's sort of like being the walking dead."*

DEVON: Yes.

OPRAH: *That you're not in control. You're not helping to cocreate your life.*

DEVON: You have to define success. I define success as peace.

OPRAH: *Me too. You're my kind of guy.*

AMY PURDY

I was born a daydreamer. So I think daydreaming just turned into visualizing. In my worst moments, in my darkest moments, is when I've done most of my visualizing. And even being here today with you was part of that vision. When I lost my legs, one of the toughest periods was when I stood up in my legs for the first time because they were so painful and they were so confining that I thought, *How am I ever going to live this life of my dreams? How am I ever going to travel the world? How am I ever going to snowboard again?* And that day, I was so emotionally and physically broken that I crawled into bed and I didn't get out for a good fifteen hours. I just lay in bed, completely mentally and emotionally exhausted. I could not wrap my head around the fact that this is my life, and I have to navigate my life with these hunks of hardware as my legs that barely move, that are so uncomfortable. And I thought, *These are my legs that I'm living in the rest of my life.* But I didn't allow myself to sit in that spot too long. I'm just not that type of person. I have to keep moving somehow.

So I hit this point where I realized, my legs are not coming back. And there is nothing I can do about this situation right now. And it was that moment that prompted me to ask myself this question: *If my life was a book, and I was the author, how would I want this story to go?* And I thought, *Well, I don't want to see myself as this sad, disabled girl. I know that. I don't want other people to see me as that either.* I thought, *What do I want to see? I want to see myself walking again gracefully.* And I wanted to see myself somehow sharing, somehow helping other people through this journey. And I saw myself snowboarding again. I had visualized it so strongly in that moment that I didn't just see myself carving down this mountain of powder. I could feel it. I could feel the wind against my face. I could feel the beat of my racing heart. I could feel my muscles twitching as if it was happening in that very moment. I didn't know *how* I was going to do it, but I knew that I was going to do it.

And now, I try to live my life knowing that if you can see it and you can feel it and you believe it, then it is completely possible.

DIANA NYAD

So I started thinking, *My mom died at eighty-two; does that mean I have only twenty-two years left?* The clock is like choking me now. And it wasn't so much what did I want to do, it was who I want to be.

At sixty, I needed to say, "Forget about the ledger. Are you in the halls of fame? Did you make some kind of money doing that?" I don't care about that anymore. As you know, those things just, as you get older ... who cares? It's, "Am I living the life that I can admire? Am I going to leave this earth a place where it's a little more than just what it was?" Those are my values. And never giving up. And finding a way through obstacles. And finding grit and will. Those are what I value.

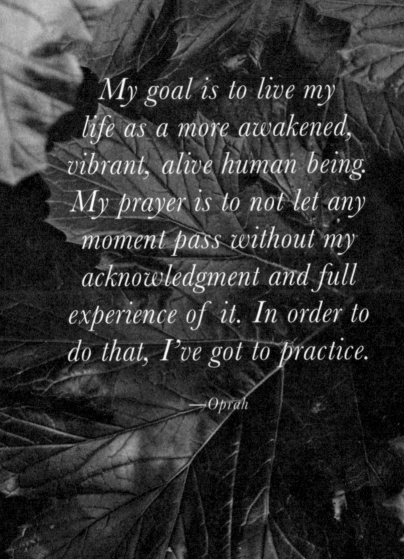

My goal is to live my life as a more awakened, vibrant, alive human being. My prayer is to not let any moment pass without my acknowledgment and full experience of it. In order to do that, I've got to practice.

—Oprah

CHAPTER THREE

MINDFULNESS

There are so many simple pleasures that allow me to delight in the present moment.

A long walk in solitude or a spirited hike with friends brings a renewed sense of gratitude and connection. I consider reading a book a sacred indulgence. And I also happen to love a cup of piping-hot masala tea. The daily ritual of being at the sink, boiling the water, steaming the milk, and then steeping the tea helps bring me to a place of stillness. Whether it's watching a sunset, or really feeling the stream of water hit your face in the shower, everyone needs to take time to find a way to quiet themselves.

Allowing these moments of awareness and recognizing that it is a magnificent thing to be alive, regardless of what might be pressing on me, has brought a level of calm that words can't adequately explain.

Many of the spiritual teachers who have talked with me on *Super Soul Sunday* describe the highest state of mindfulness as a "constant state of prayer." This means acknowledging only what you are experiencing in that moment. The true power of staying in the *now* means that you resist projecting what might happen in the future or lamenting past mistakes. There will always be times of stress or sadness, but when you feel the earth moving, that's the time to bring yourself back to center. Whatever shake-up or disturbance that might come, you'll handle that when it actually happens. But in this moment, you're still breathing. In this moment, you've survived. In this moment, you're finding a way to step onto higher ground.

Today and every day, I continue to do the consciousness work, focusing on prayer and just being still. I awaken, and my first thought is, *Thank you*, and my next thought is, *I'm still here in this body*. I feel the *All* that is God so deeply that it lifts and carries me. Sometimes I actually feel weightless in the love that I call God, because I sense it in all things.

The entry point for living consciously is mindfulness. Let the words and examples on the following pages be your guide to becoming more relaxed, responding to the inevitable swirl around you with compassion.

Staying present is the reason, after talking to thousands of people over the years, I still have *aha* moments. Meaningful things happen when you release the anxious thoughts and negative chatter in your head and tune in to what the person in front of you is saying. Slowing down, showing up, and listening to your child, spouse, parent, or friend shows them they have been seen and heard by you. Not only are you providing validation when they need it most, you are consciously creating your own spiritual practice.

—*Oprah*

JON KABAT-ZINN

OPRAH: *Is mindfulness science? Is it art? Is it spiritual?*

JON KABAT-ZINN: It's a gateway into the full dimensionality of being human and being alive.

OPRAH: *Oh, I love that. "It's a gateway into the full dimensionality of being human." And without it, you're missing out.*

JON: Well, you're missing a lot. You know, if you miss the look in your child's eye one day, you've missed it. If you missed the look in your lover's eyes the next day, you've missed that. If you miss the beauty of sitting under trees, well, you've missed that. If you sum that over many moments, many years, you may wind up missing the most beautiful aspects of your own life. Who are you going to blame for that? I was too busy? Well, who was too busy? Who tells oneself, "I don't have any time," when all you've got is time? All you've got is this moment. And we might as well take it while we're alive, because sooner or later, we're going to be dead. So the perfect moment is this one.

SHONDA RHIMES

My daughter, Harper, is thirteen. She's very different from me. Very different. She is an extroverted, tall, thin, beautiful, actress kind of child. And if you put me in a corner with a book for the rest of my life, I would be happy. We are polar opposites. And I have really spent my time thinking this year, *How do I embrace her personality and make her shine for who she is?* And that has been really wonderful for her and for me—as opposed to me thinking, *How do I get her to fit into the box of what I think a kid is supposed to be?*

And so I said *yes* to my kids in a way that I had never done before. My other daughter says to me all the time, "Wanna play? Wanna play?" And there are so many times I've said, "Well, I can't right now, honey, I'm doing this. I can't right now." I decided that every single time she said to me, "Wanna play?" I would say, "Yes."

So it doesn't matter if I'm wearing an evening gown and heading out to the DGA [Directors Guild of America] Awards or I have my bags on my shoulder and I'm heading out to work, I drop everything I'm doing, I get down on my hands and knees, and we play. And, you know, she's three. It's ten minutes. And she loves it. And it's changed my sense of being a mother and my sense of pride in being a mother.

And it's changed our relationship.

ARIANNA HUFFINGTON

Because I'm this obsessive, type A personality, I had to really get a bad wake-up call. I mean, thank God not bad enough to be life threatening. But I actually collapsed from exhaustion on April 6, 2007, two years after I founded the Huffington Post. I hit my head on my desk, broke my cheekbone, and got four stitches on my right eye. I was very lucky I didn't lose my eye. Then in a way what was worse, is I had to go from doctor to doctor, from MRI to echocardiogram to find out what was wrong with me. Did I have a brain tumor? They didn't know what was wrong.

And they discovered there was nothing medically wrong with me, but just about everything wrong with the way I was leading my life and what I was prioritizing. And waiting—you know, doctors' waiting rooms are great places to ask life's big questions.

And so, I was asking myself, *Is this success?* By conventional definitions of success, I was successful. By any sane definition of success, if you are lying in your own pool of blood on your office floor, you're not successful. The most important thing I want people to get is that there is no trade-off.

RUSSELL SIMMONS

If you sit, and the thoughts settle, and the noise disappears, then you see all God's beauty. Those people who are fully awake see all the sunsets. You drive your car, you see every flower. It promotes a lasting, stable, happy relationship with the world. And so if you meditate, you'll be a happier, more stable person. You will be more productive. Because if you're awake and present and thoughtful, you're good at your job. And you're a good giver. And also, having that kind of focus, that single point of focus it takes when you're working and when you're engaged, is the real thing that promotes happiness on its own. And then the things come as a result.

The best way to be in the present moment is to be aware that you're not in the moment. As soon as you're aware that you're not in the moment, you're in the moment.

—*Deepak Chopra*

Father RICHARD ROHR

I try to preserve good chunks of silence. If I can do that and learn how to rest there, it is a resting, then I have to use that as a touchstone all day. Can I get back to that place of who I am in God apart from my role, my success, my title, my authorship, or all of those things? Those are going to pass. And silence is the one spiritual discipline that is found in all of the world religions at the higher levels. Some degree of silence. And that would be my practice. Finding inner silence and then honoring the silence that's really around everything.

RAINN WILSON

RAINN WILSON: I definitely knew I wanted to be an actor. I had that dream; I had that longing to be an artist, and that was my deepest drive.

OPRAH: *Because the heart of our soul's calling is that longing you're talking about.*

RAINN: Yes. And I knew that I basically had to be an actor or I would die. I had such a deep drive to become an actor. And at the same time, you know, I grew up as a member of the Bahá'í Faith and my parents are Bahá'ís. It's always difficult to sum up a world religion in a nutshell. But essentially the Bahá'í Faith is a religion of unity.

OPRAH: *So you grew up with this sense of openness toward all religions and a belief that helped you realize we're all the same. We're all connected.*

RAINN: So to grow up feeling that we're all one human family, to know that from as soon as you could think, or walk, or talk was a gift.

OPRAH: *And so I'm sure that infuses not only your personality but also distinctly infuses your art.*

RAINN: An interesting thing about the Bahá'í Faith is that in this day and age, Bahá'u'lláh tells us that the making of art is no different than prayer.

OPRAH: *I love that. I love that.*

RAINN: There's not any difference between lifting up a paintbrush and touching it to a canvas and bowing your head in a church.

OPRAH: *The hairs on my head rose a little bit when you said that. I got a little tingle from that, Rainn. That art is prayer, creativity is an expression of prayer. It is prayer.*

NORMAN LEAR

OPRAH: *You write that when we laugh together, we are one. How does laughter elevate the human experience?*

NORMAN LEAR: I believe my longevity has depended a great deal on the amount of laughter I've had in my life. You know, I love thinking about this. I could cry thinking about this. You stand behind an audience, as I did time and again when Archie Bunker was at his funniest, let's say. When an audience laughs together, every seat, you know, side by side, they tend to rise up and out of their chairs a little and down and then back up again.

OPRAH: *Really. I never thought about that before. You're right.*

NORMAN: And if there's anything more spiritual in our life, an audience moving on a belly laugh, I mean, that's praying, that's gratitude, that's enjoyment.

OPRAH: *Yeah. I never thought of it until you said that; it's your offering.*

NORMAN: Yes.

OPRAH: *It's your praise.*

IYANLA VANZANT

IYANLA VANZANT: Here's the lesson. When you find yourself in a new situation, a new circumstance, a new life experience, everything that requires healing is going to rush to the surface.

OPRAH: *Whoo!*

IYANLA: And if you don't take a minute to breathe, to gather yourself, to pray, you will do what you've always done.

OPRAH: *Yes.*

IYANLA: So you got to be clear enough, grounded enough, centered enough to say, "How am I going to handle it this time?"

OPRAH: *So the lesson is pause …*

IYANLA: We go from being twenty to thirty without a pause. We go from one job to the next, from one bed to the next. For every one, pause. Take a breath. Pause.

OPRAH: *Women make this mistake over and over and over again with relationships. And men, too.*

IYANLA: Yes.

OPRAH: *You get out of one and you go into the next and you are now into the next one, because it looks different or looks bigger or the grass is greener. You think that it's different, and you bring all your old stuff to it.*

IYANLA: It took me forty years to realize that I was trying to get my father's approval and acceptance. One man: forty years. And I kept reliving my issues with my father.

OPRAH: *Over and over.*

IYANLA: Over and over. One day my soul just opened up, and the Holy Spirit said, "You can't get your daddy to love you like that." So that's when I had to take a pause and look at it. And it's the truth, Oprah. Facing the truth is hard. It is painful as hell. Excuse me, Sunday.

OPRAH: *Excuse us, Super Soul …*

IYANLA: The truth will set you free, but you have to endure the labor pains of birthing it.

MICHAEL SINGER

OPRAH: *Speaking for myself, I want to be able to be connected to that seat of the self that is ultimately where the power of God flows through. How do we begin to make that happen for ourselves?*

MICHAEL SINGER: All you have to do is get to the point in your everyday life, every moment of life is a spiritual experience, and I know you know that, right?

OPRAH: *Yes, I do. That's why we're here on* Super Soul Sunday.

MICHAEL: And the reason it becomes a spiritual experience is because you've realized you are causing the vast majority of your own problems, due to your mental reactions. So as life unfolds on a daily basis, you have the right to choose not to do that. You can still go to work, you still take care of the kids, you just lean away from this mess that the mind is doing to amplify and overemphasize or overexaggerate whatever's going on.

OPRAH: *And then what do we do? Lean into what that awareness is saying?*

MICHAEL: What will happen is when you let go of the noisy mind, you will end up in a seat of quiet, because that's what it is back there: quiet.

OPRAH: *Is stillness, stillness.*

MICHAEL: And my experience is that now you can look at reality and you will know what to do.

OPRAH: *Yes. I think what we're all ultimately seeking, even when we don't know it, when I would ask people on the show for years, "What do you want?" everybody would say they want happiness. But aren't we all ultimately seeking freedom?*

MICHAEL: Yes. We're seeking a state of absolute well-being, and that's what freedom means. Right?

OPRAH: *That's what it means. Yeah!*

MICHAEL: And what's beautiful, is the true freedom is freedom *from* yourself, not freedom *for* yourself.

ANNE LAMOTT

ANNE LAMOTT: It's very easy for me to see God in my backyard with the dogs and with the very bitter cat that I call my own. But when someone's sick, when you get the bad phone call, when someone's heard from the doctor, when the appearance of life is very, very shaky, it throws me completely off my game. It throws me for a loop. I think, *This can't be right.*

OPRAH: *And I know you believe that we can pray anytime, anywhere.*

ANNE: Anytime, and you can say anything. I say to God sometimes, "You have got to be kidding." Or I say, "Would it be so much skin off Your nose to cut this person a little slack?" And I think you can say anything. You can say, "I'm mad at You. And I'm not going to be a good sport about it. How about that?" And that's prayer. Silence can be prayer. Rage can be prayer. It's truth. It's all prayer. When we are talking to something that the rest of the world may not be seeing right then and when we're talking from the deepest part of our hearts, we're trying to tell the truth. That's prayer.

Dr. JILL BOLTE TAYLOR

DR. JILL BOLTE TAYLOR: Pay attention to how things feel in your body. Because you know what you feel like in your body when you get angry. And you have a choice when you get angry of either being angry or of paying attention to what it feels like in your body when you are angry. And when you have that kind of a physiological response when you get angry, it only takes ninety seconds. It takes ninety seconds from the moment you feel that trigger happen, and you feel yourself starting to get angry, for the chemicals to flush through your body and then flush completely out of you. Ninety seconds is all.

OPRAH: *So start timing it?*

JILL: Start timing it. Within ninety seconds, it will be gone, and you'll go, "Okay, I just dodged that one."

OPRAH: *Okay, then why do people harbor the same feelings for years?*

JILL: Because they keep rethinking the same thought that restimulates that emotional circuitry, and they rerun the loop.

OPRAH: *Got it.*

JILL: And hook right back into that hostility. People can stay angry for days, and weeks, and years. It's phenomenal. Just because they're choosing, either consciously or unconsciously, they're choosing to rerun the loops, the circuitry.

ZAINAB SALBI

I actually always thought that I am not a beautiful woman. I would look at myself in the mirror, and no matter how many people, my former husband, everyone was like, "You're beautiful." Nope. I would look and say, "I'm not a beautiful woman." And one day, you know, a Tibetan woman actually told me, "You need to start meditating on your eyes." So I go to the mirror—same mirror, by the way—and I'm meditating and I started looking into the pupil of my eyes. I just kept on meditating on it, and I saw my soul. And it was like, "Wow, that's a beautiful person inside." And little by little, I started seeing my own beauty and stopped judging myself.

THICH NHAT HANH

THICH NHAT HANH: If you are fully present in the here and the now, you need only to make a step or take a breath in order to enter the kingdom of God. Happiness is possible in the here and the now. And once you have touched the kingdom, you don't need to run after objects of your craving, like power, fame, sensual pleasure, and so on.

OPRAH: *What if in this moment of mindfulness you are being challenged? Do you go to your breath then, or do you just not resist this challenging situation? What is the first thing you do?*

THICH NHAT HANH: All you have to do is breathe mindfully and recognize the feeling. You recognize the situation and help yourself not be overwhelmed by the negative feeling like fear or anxiety. You are still yourself. It's like a mother: When the baby is crying, she picks up the baby and she holds the baby tenderly in her arms. Your pain, your anxiety is your baby. You have to take care of it. You have to go back to yourself, recognize the suffering in you, embrace the suffering, and you get relief. And if you continue with your practice of mindfulness and concentration, you understand the roots, the nature of that ill-being, and you know the way to transform it.

Your life is always
speaking to you.
The fundamental
spiritual question is:
Will you listen?

—*Oprah*

CHAPTER FOUR

SPIRITUAL GPS

The meaning of *wisdom* for me is recognizing the moment when what you *know* aligns perfectly with what you *feel*.

That powerful flash of clarity telling you the right decision to make originates from only one source: You. (Notice the capital Y). There is the little *you*—your personality. And the greater *You* spelled with a capital Y—your soul.

The people you love and trust most will hopefully always be there to offer advice. But you are on your own journey, responsible for charting your own course. Whenever I have felt most tested, lost, or unsure of my own direction, these words from "Invictus" that I memorized at eight years old have been a way forward.

I am the master of my fate.
I am the captain of my soul.

With every decision, you are steering your own ship. Beneath all of those protective layers built up between you and the world lives an inner voice that goes by many names. Some call it *instinct* or *intuition*.

I call that persistent "knowing" our spiritual GPS. It acts as our internal compass, designed to help you move through life no matter what distractions or obstacles get in your way. Your GPS is always turned on. Whether you're headed on the right track or about to take a destructive turn, your emotional guidance system lets you know. Each quote you read in the following pages offers a different tool or real-life experience intended to help you tune in more sharply to what your spirit, your GPS, is trying to tell you.

Every right decision I've ever made has come from listening to my gut. Every wrong decision was a result of me dismissing the small, still voice within me. Your life speaks to you in whispers— that little nudge saying, "Hmm, something doesn't feel right." If you ignore it, the whispers turn into pebbles thrown at you, warning, "There's a problem. Danger ahead!" If those signs remain unexamined, you will inevitably experience what feels like a heavy brick to the head. Shutting out the brick guarantees disaster will strike. You will see your life come crashing down like a brick wall. I've seen this happen so often in my own life, I now try to respond immediately, at the first whisper.

What every one of these *Super Soul Sunday* conversations has taught me is that no matter who you are, if you've been faking your way through life, ignoring your inner compass, the wake-up call can be harsh; job loss, the end of a relationship, money problems, disruption in any form. No matter how devastating, these are opportunities to stop sleepwalking through your life, wake up, and pay attention to the red flags, whispers, pebbles, and bricks along the way.

Your real purpose on Earth is to become more of who you really are—to live to the highest degree what is pure, what is honest, what is natural, what feels like the real you.

You'll know you've found it when every cell in your body vibrates with your own truth. When you're filled up by what you're doing instead of being drained by it.

Follow your instincts. That's where true wisdom unfolds.

—Oprah

MICHAEL BERNARD

BECKWITH

OPRAH: *Let's talk about vibration. You use it a lot in your teaching. And I don't know when it was I first understood that there is an energy and a frequency to everything. And that your whole role and goal in life is to line up with whatever is the frequency that is going to allow you to move in the flow of your own life.*

MICHAEL BERNARD BECKWITH: Exactly. We are vibrational beings. You know, we're not just flesh and blood. If you put anything under a microscope, you're going to ultimately see that everything is vibration. And as the scientists are now telling us, there's information there. But it's not solid. It's always moving. So we're vibrational beings. So as you were just saying, when we lift our vibration to what we want to experience, it happens first on a vibratory level, and then it shows up and manifests in our life. So people who are holding on to rancor, animosity, they're slowing down their vibration.

OPRAH: *I just had an* aha *there. You're saying, when you recognize your vibrational frequency, you're drawing into yourself all the time, literally, the vibration that is most like what you're putting out.*

MICHAEL: Right. Another way of saying it is you cannot have what you're not willing to become vibrationally. You see? This is why people that win the lottery, they lose everything. They'll finally get the person they think they want to be with and they can't keep the relationship. Or they'll get a modicum of success but can't hold on to it. Because inside, they weren't vibrationally aligned. They really hadn't become it. So you can temporarily manipulate and get things. But to have it completely, you have to lift your vibration and become that in the vibration. You're not attracting things to you. You're radiating. You're radiating from within, out. So if I become the vibrational frequency of love, harmony, peace, and I'm radiating that, it's going to show up in my life.

OPRAH: *That's the key. That's the word. You're not attracting it. You have to be it and radiate it, and then it is drawn to you. And you to it. So then the work becomes about you working on yourself.*

MICHAEL: You have to like yourself. I mean, when you're by yourself, you have to look at those thoughts, the beautiful thoughts, the crazy thoughts. You have to embrace yourself, you have to forgive yourself, you have to love yourself. And when you can fall in love with yourself and like yourself when you're by yourself, now you can be with others. But if you don't like yourself when you're by your-self, then you're pulling on others to make you happy.

CAROLINE MYSS

CAROLINE MYSS: And if you saw everything about your life as a learning, as a lesson … "I'm looking for truth." "Does this drain power?" "Am I empowering?" With every choice I make, I'm either choosing to grace somebody or withhold it, to give power or to take it back. If people understand that with every single choice, "I'm either going to learn something from this or I'm not."

OPRAH: *So every single choice we make is either going to enhance the spirit or it's going to drain the spirit?*

CAROLINE: There is nothing in between.

OPRAH: *Another way to say that is you're either walking in the direction of love or you're walking away from it. You're walking to fear, right?*

CAROLINE: Totally. And there is no other choice. Even if you're in a grocery store and you're thinking, *Should I buy this or not?* And your gut says, *You know you can't eat that,* and you decide, I'm not going to listen to that voice. Right there, even in that tiny thing, you've walked toward fear. Because you've blocked your intuitive voice.

OPRAH: *So every day, in the smallest of ways and the largest of ways, we're either giving ourselves power or taking away from it.*

CAROLINE: That's right.

OPRAH: *So how do you know when you are on the right path? Which dream belongs to you, or what husband belongs to you, or what job belongs to you?*

CAROLINE: Okay, here's your clue. You're not put in a position to betray yourself. You don't betray yourself anymore. You're not put in a position where you feel like you have to negotiate your sense of integrity, which is an act of betrayal. You don't feel like you have to compromise who you are.

OPRAH: *I got that. It's like, if you're at a job, you know you're really gifted and talented. People are not paying you for what you value yourself to be. You come into work every day feeling like,* I'm really not valued. I'm not being respected for what I do. *Or,* My boss is unkind, *or whatever the situation might be, there's an unease with you. And so when you have more respect for yourself, put yourself in a position where you can feel your sense of value or worth, that turns around. And that's how you know.*

CAROLINE: You know because you don't feel like, This isn't costing me my power. This isn't costing me my psyche. This isn't costing me my soul. I don't feel confused on some deep level. I'm not drained. I can be tired after a day's work, but I'm not psychically drained where I feel like I'm losing life.

CHERYL STRAYED

When my mother died, it brought me to what I think of as my most savage self. My mother was the taproot of my life, and suddenly I didn't have that anymore, and I had a wild love for my mother. I had wild sorrow. And then I went wild into my life. I think so much of where I began this journey is—I keep using this word—lost. I didn't know where I was. I didn't know where to place myself. I think, too, so much of this goes back to that essential primal need that we all have to feel that we belong. And our first definition of how we belong is given to us through our mother and our father. And I didn't have either of those people anymore. And so who was I, and where was I? I was just lost in that Milky Way. And so when I felt myself located, that was the beginning of my rebirth and my sense of redefinition of my place in the world.

President JIMMY CARTER

OPRAH: *You've said that you're a praying man, and you never prayed more than you did when you were in the White House. What is your fervent prayer? What is the prayer that resides in your heart?*

PRESIDENT CARTER: That I can use the best of my talent and ability and influence to enhance the kingdom of God on Earth, which I believe comprises peace and freedom and the alleviation of suffering, human rights.

OPRAH: *A lot of people right now feel like they have the weight of the world on their shoulders. They feel burdened. But when you are president of the United States, you literally have the weight of the world on your shoulders. Did you feel that?*

PRESIDENT CARTER: I did.

OPRAH: *Were you constantly aware of that?*

PRESIDENT CARTER: Yes, I always knew that I had the biggest military force in the world and more influence in economics and politics and culture than perhaps any other human being on Earth. And I wanted to use it wisely and with a maximum possible element of humility. And be aware of how my decisions could affect other people for the better or worse.

OPRAH: *So what role did your faith play in all of your works?*

PRESIDENT CARTER: I tried to put my faith into practical applications when I was in the White House.

OPRAH: *When was it tested the most, your faith?*

PRESIDENT CARTER: When the hostages were being held and when I was urged by almost all of my advisers, including my wife, that I should take military action against Iran. And I felt that my Christian faith called on me to avoid using military action when I didn't have to. And I was lucky that when I was president, we never dropped a bomb, we never fired a missile, we never shot a bullet.

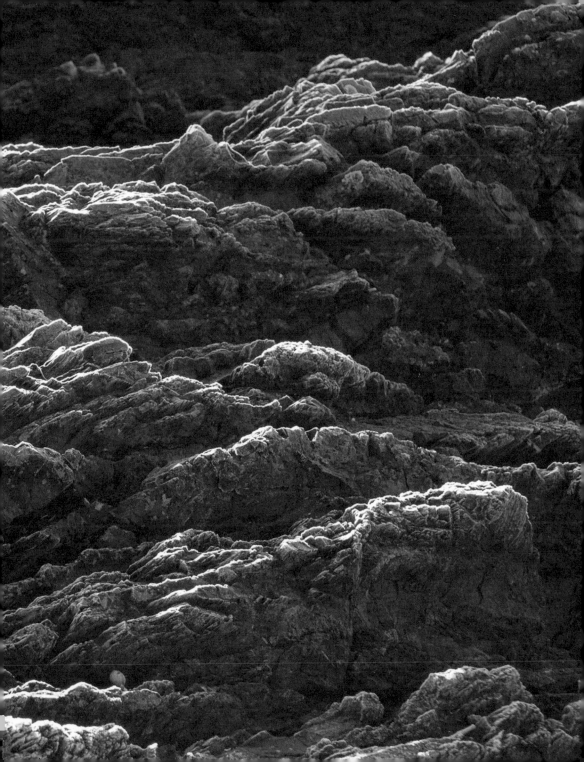

I believe everyone has a God-size hole inside of them that we try to fill with shopping or with a relationship or food or sex or drugs. But it's not out there. It's in here. It's an internal connection. And that's what a spiritual practice, listening to your intuition, having a creative expression, being of service is all about. That is how you sustainably fill up your God-size hole. Otherwise, it's like a drop that's disconnected from the ocean. You just wither and die.

—*Mastin Kipp*

ELIZABETH GILBERT

OPRAH: *So was it just this unsettling with yourself that was unraveling in the marriage?*

ELIZABETH GILBERT: It was a combination of things, incompatibilities that had occurred, but I won't lay that on him. Because the reality is that it was much more of an internal volcano than it was anything else.

OPRAH: *For you?*

ELIZABETH: Yes. I had woken up to the fact that my life no longer resembled me and that it was only going to get worse.

OPRAH: *Oh, your life no longer resembled you. Let's just hold that a moment. "My life no longer resembled me."*

ELIZABETH: It didn't look like me. I had friends who came to my house and said, "I can't believe you live in this house." And I would say, "No, it's great. I'm really happy." You know, but it's not. And the deal-breaker was that we were talking about having kids. And I think one thing that had happened as I had advanced on the trail toward marriage is something that happens to a lot of women, which was that I was ambivalent. In many of these key moments of my life, I felt ambivalence.

It was an equal yes and no. I want to do this, I don't want to do this. I didn't want to hold up the train of progress, so I just always said yes.

OPRAH: *Yes.*

ELIZABETH: And I never knew at that age, in my twenties, that "I don't know" is actually a legitimate answer that you're allowed to say. You're allowed to say, "I don't know," and you're allowed to ask for as much time as you need until you do know. And if somebody doesn't want to give you that time, they're allowed to leave. But you're allowed to sit with your "I don't know."

And I never sat with it because it was uncomfortable. Nobody likes that place. And so I always said yes. "Oh, sure. Let's move in together, let's get married, let's buy a house, let's do all this stuff …" that I was sort of half yes, half no. And when it came to "Let's have a kid," that's where I thought, *I cannot make that decision from a place of yes and no. That has to be a yes or it can't happen.*

MARIANNE WILLIAMSON

OPRAH: *The one thing that lived in me was when you said, "We were either walking in the direction of love or the direction of fear." And I got that so deeply that it really transformed me. That there really are only two emotions. And for the rest of my life I always recognize when I'm walking in the direction of love and the direction of fear. And the book passage from you that I love the most and that has been quoted the most is "Our deepest fear is not that we are inadequate. Our deepest fear is that we are powerful beyond measure." So when you wrote that, it came from what part of yourself?*

MARIANNE WILLIAMSON: Part of that is this fear that we might offend somebody else. That somehow if I have, then you have less, rather than realizing that if I'm living in the light of my own true being, it actually subconsciously liberates you to live from the light of your true being. You know, what's true in the material world is the exact opposite of what's true in the spiritual world. So in the material world, there are only so many pieces of the pie. If I have a piece of the pie, you have less. But in the spiritual world, the more I'm able to actualize—and that's what enlightenment is; it's self-actualization, actualizing the love that is in our hearts—the more there is a field of possibility for others. I mean, look at your career as an example.

OPRAH: *And that is true for every person.*

MARIANNE: Every person.

SUE MONK KIDD

SUE MONK KIDD: The soul often speaks, at least for me, through longing. It manifests like a restlessness. And when the soul longs, it's trying to tell you something. And I think the soul speaks through what pulls us. That allure. The longing. The restlessness.

OPRAH: *Yes. There are so many people who can relate to this. I remember when I was a young reporter in Baltimore and every day I would get up and I'd go out and cover the stories, and I was on the news, and it felt so out of alignment for me. I always knew that there was something more for me to do because my friend Gayle—we met working there—she loved it. She felt so at home with it. She was so inquisitive and curious and loved it. And for me, it felt like I'm in the wrong space. I'm wondering if, when you were a nurse, which is such an honorable calling, and*

for people who are supposed to be doing that, nobody can do it better. Did you feel out of alignment being a nurse? As I felt being a reporter?

SUE: I did. I felt that I was not in my place of belonging. And that is a big thing for me, to be in my place of belonging.

OPRAH: *Oh, that's so good. We all are looking for, Where do I belong?*

SUE: What do I belong to? I mean, what is faith if not paying attention to what we belong to?

OPRAH: *Yes.*

SUE: When I was a nurse, which is the most noble thing in the world, I wanted it to work. But I felt out of line. I felt like I wasn't in that place of belonging. And it just took me a while to return.

TIMOTHY SHRIVER

Normal. The tyranny of that word, it's just, like, it's a cancer in the culture. Are you normal? Are you fitting in? Are you like everyone else? My God, it's terrifying. And yet we all feel that. So we come to these Special Olympic Games expecting to be sad. We come to them expecting to feel pity. We say things like, "There but for the grace of God go I." People say that well intentioned to me all the time. And I always want to say to them, "You know, that pity, that fear that embodies that idea of 'I'm healthy and they're not,' I think there's a strength that only vulnerability knows." You know? And I think the answer of our Special Olympic athletes is, there is only power in vulnerability and trust. The other power is superficial. It locks people up. It puts people behind bars. Social. Cultural. Political. Interpersonal. There is only power.

You know, I grew up, everybody's in the spotlight. That's where we all wanted to get to. That's where you'd be successful. And what I saw was sometimes, when the lights are the brightest, people feel the most invisible. I think sometimes where you think you want to go is not the place where you will find your most heartfelt, most meaningful, most purposeful life. I mean, I looked around thinking I wanted to be like all those people in lights, and I found myself happiest in places nobody wanted to be.

Ego is an imposter,
imposing on the real you,
making you think you are
something that you're not.
True self-esteem is realizing
that the stillness and
presence in me is the same as
the presence in all people.

—*Oprah*

CHAPTER FIVE

EGO

The conversations I've shared with renowned thought leader and spiritual teacher Eckhart Tolle have been some of the most meaningful of my life.

His wisdom has been so transformative, I keep a copy of his book *A New Earth* on my bedside table.

I didn't understand the true meaning of ego until I met Eckhart.

I used to think that ego only presented itself as arrogance, selfishness, or feelings of superiority. But I know now that it's not always someone who is acting out or showing off. Everyone has an ego. And I believe most people aren't even aware of how it affects their daily life.

Understanding the ego's constant disruption to our spiritual development is such an integral lesson in our path to awareness that it has become one of my very favorite topics to discuss on *Super Soul Sunday*. If you watch the show regularly, you will almost always hear me ask, "What role does the ego play in this situation?" This is the essential question we should all be asking ourselves whenever we encounter difficulty. As you read the words of wisdom selected for this chapter, you will begin to understand how the answer is universal:

The ego has the power to influence or derail *every* aspect of our lives.

Accepting this as truth opens the door to where the real work begins.

It was Eckhart who opened my eyes to how an ego-based mind can dominate everything. Ego represents that part of ourselves that identifies with our self-image, personality, talents, accomplishments, and perceived weaknesses—everything that encompasses the false self.

The ego draws a line and separates you from everyone else. It leads you to see the world as "this is me and this is the other," when, in fact, we all share the same source of spiritual energy. The ego makes judgments and longs to feel special. It loves conflict, creates enemies, and operates out of fear. In those moments, if you call your false self out by saying, "Oh, that's my ego flaring up," you begin to diminish its power. You begin to recognize that you are not your past, your social status, or the shape of your body. The size of your bank account has no bearing on your true self.

What these conversations have taught me is that as we realize our own spiritual evolution, we have the miraculous ability to shed our current state of ego. As Eckhart Tolle says, the ego cannot exist in consciousness.

—*Oprah*

ECKHART TOLLE

OPRAH: *Have you lost your ego?*

ECKHART TOLLE: Yes.

OPRAH: *You have completely?*

ECKHART: Well, let's see. Who knows? Tomorrow it may suddenly appear again. You let me know if it does, because I wouldn't know it if it's really the ego.

OPRAH: *This is one of my favorite quotes of yours: "You do not become good by trying to be good, but by finding the goodness that is already within you and allowing that goodness to emerge." Again we're talking about going to presence, the divine within you, and bringing that forth to whatever it is you do.*

ECKHART: Yes. Because trying to be good is often to improve one's self-image.

OPRAH: *Right. That's ego-driven.*

ECKHART: Ultimately, it's ego. For example, some people have been trying for centuries to love their neighbor as themselves. But they have been finding it difficult because loving your neighbor as yourself really means, first of all, you need to be in touch with yourself, the self that you are beyond the form. And then you can love your neighbor

as yourself because you recognize your oneness with your neighbor.

OPRAH: *Yes. And so what you're saying is so beautiful. I get it. Lots of bing-bing ahas here. You're not saying love your neighbor as yourself —not as yourself the personality. It doesn't mean give your neighbor tickets to the theater or whatever. It means the deeper inner-self. The higher self.*

ECKHART: Yes. So I call love the recognizing yourself in the other, and yourself your essential self. Then, when I meet people and interact with people, I see them on two levels or feel them on two levels. On one level, they are the form, which is the body and their psychological makeup. On another level, they are the consciousness that I also am, that pure essence.

OPRAH: *You see that in every person that you encounter?*

ECKHART: Yes. And that makes it much easier to interact with people and much more pleasant, because sometimes the personality, the psychological makeup, is not that wonderful. And then one is able to let that go, because you can sense beyond that there is an essence to that human being.

WAYNE DYER

WAYNE DYER: The first nine months of your life, going back to your conception.

OPRAH: *You trusted God for everything.*

WAYNE: Everything. You didn't say, "Oh my God, I hope I get a nose, and I hope it shows up in the right place." You were completely into surrender. Then you come out after the ninth month, and you get surrounded by people who say, "That's really good work, God, really good work. We'll take over from here." And the minute you start taking over from here, you develop an ego, which is where you edge God out. E-G-O, you edge God out.

OPRAH: *Oh, I never heard it that way before. That is so good.*

WAYNE: Yes. So you edge God out, and you just push that to the side. And what is this ego, what is it? It's an idea, Oprah. That's all it is. It's an idea that we carry around. The ego says, "I am what I have, I am what I do, I am what other people think of me. I'm separate from everybody else. I'm separate from what's missing in my life, and I'm separate from God." Those are the six components of the ego, and that's what we're raised on and what we're trained on. Meantime, we showed up here, we didn't have to do a thing.

The wounded ego must hide all that we believe is unacceptable about ourselves. To accomplish this task, it constructs a mask to prove to others that we are not as defective, inferior, worthless, and bad as we might fear we are. None of us likes to admit that we have these flaws and insecurities, so to hide them, we create a persona at a very young age. We start to wrap ourselves up in a new package that we believe will bring us the love, attention, and acceptance that we hunger for. We create personas so that we can belong.

—*Debbie Ford*

BRENÉ BROWN

BRENÉ BROWN: To me, I call the ego the hustler. He's my hustler. And the ego says to me, "You have no inherent worth. You got to hustle for it, baby." How fast are you going to run? How high are you going to jump? How many likes do you have? How many comments do you have on that post? That's the hustle.

OPRAH: *And isn't it we now live in a culture that measures itself, ourselves, by how many likes we get?*

BRENÉ: For sure. We are in a scarcity culture. Never enough. Never good enough, thin enough, rich enough, safe enough, certain enough. And what I think is interesting is, I wanted to get your thought on this just because you've also been looking in the faces of people for many years, right?

OPRAH: *Yes.*

BRENÉ: I started my research six months before 9/11. I would say the past twelve years have been marked by a deep fear in our culture. It's like a collective post-traumatic response.

OPRAH: *Oh my God, I just had a big aha.*

BRENÉ: I love it! What?

OPRAH: *When you just said that, I just realized that we shifted from being on alert and afraid of whether it's the orange code or the yellow code. We somehow internalized that fear, and it shows up as the bickering and the snarkiness. We have internalized the fear so we're not worried about what the code alert is anymore, but that fear has been internalized. That's what I heard you saying.*

BRENÉ: That's exactly it.

Dr. SHEFALI TSABARY

The way the parenting paradigm has been set up is just designed for even a greater boost of ego than I've ever seen in any other relationship. And how does the ego sound? It's *my*. It's *I*. Correct? We start talking like this. I, as a parent; my child. Right? The possession. The ownership. It's inherent. That's why I love this relationship, because it's such a trick from the Universe. You know? The Universe gives you children. It says they're yours. So it seduces you into thinking, *It's mine. You have to call them mine.* Right? *I'm not wrong in saying mine.* But yet the child comes out and says, "I'm not you. I'm not you. I'm not you. Now deal with me. Attune to me. Do you recognize my spirit? I will not belong or be yours. I can come through you, but I will not be yours."

   You cannot even dare to have the audacity to think about raising another being until you yourself are parented. Until you have raised your own self to the highest level of evolution. Then you can aspire

to meet this being who is living in the present who has no attachment to identity. I tell parents, "You have to own that there's a big degree, a high amount of narcissism, egoic desire to fulfill your own self to have children." Parenting is not selfless. There are elements of selflessness in it. But the driving force to have a child comes from your own desire to complete something within you. If you don't raise yourself first, and parent yourself, then you will aspire to make your child a mini version of yourself. So you're actually not even raising the child then. You're just raising yourself. So let's just call it what it is. Rein that ego in, parent yourself, and then you will attune to your child. Then you will make space for the spirit of your child to unfold.

JACK CANFIELD

Every time we are negative about someone else, we are actually affecting ourselves. And the other thing that's important is every time you judge someone else, it's just a projection of our own self-judgment. Parts of ourselves we don't accept. Parts of ourselves we won't give permission to express. And so basically, the old thing when you're pointing your finger, there's three fingers pointing back. And so I always tell people that whatever you focus on, you get more of. So if I'm gossiping about someone that I'm judging or being negative about, then I'm actually creating more negativity inside of me, and I'm not focusing on what I want.

JEFF WEINER

OPRAH: *There was an article that came out about you, about your evolution, that* Fortune *magazine did a while back, and you were described as someone who "wielded your fierce intelligence like a blunt instrument." And when you read that, you felt what?*

JEFF WEINER: I think when I was a younger executive, I had a tendency to make the same mistake that a lot of inexperienced executives make, which is projecting onto your team the way you do things and expecting them to do things the way you do them. And when there's any kind of dissonance, when someone's not doing things the way you expect them to be done, you can get frustrated.

And you express that frustration. And it's a mistake. It was through an interaction I had with my own manager where I was expressing that I felt they were not managing compassionately that I realized I was actually doing the exact same thing with someone on my team.

OPRAH: *This is a good story. You're in a meeting, and somebody's being a jerk and constantly being passive-aggressive.*

JEFF: So we would get together a team of leaders as a part of the staff meeting for this individual, and here was a colleague of mine, a member of this person's team, who was very effective in their role, but they weren't doing the job the way our manager wanted them to do the job. And so it would frustrate them to no end, and they would make jokes at this person's expense. They would undermine them in front of the team. And I remember thinking, *This is not good for the individual.* It wasn't good for my boss, and it wasn't good for us as a team. So we would have one-on-ones every now and again, and I said, "Hey, I've got to give you some feedback." I said, "The next time you feel like making a joke at this person's expense or you get frustrated and let them know in front of all of us, you should go find a mirror and express that frustration to yourself.

Because you're the reason they're in the role. And if you don't like the way they're doing their job, take the time to coach them. And if they're not capable of doing the job the way you believe they should be able to do the job, find another role for them. And if that's not going to work out, then transition them and do it in a way that's compassionate and constructive." And a couple of weeks later, we reconvened. And he said, "I have to thank you for your advice." As he's saying this, I realized I was doing the exact same thing to someone on my team. The exact same thing. And so in that moment, I vowed that as long as I was going to be responsible for managing other people, I was going to aspire to manage compassionately, where I wasn't necessarily trying to have them do things the way I did them. But I was putting myself in their shoes, understanding what motivated them, their hopes, their dreams, their fears, and trying to lead as effectively as possible.

OPRAH: *So compassionate leadership is getting to the heart and soul of what a company really is.*

PEMA CHÖDRÖN

PEMA CHÖDRÖN: A lot of people I've encountered, the losing the job, the failure coming in any kind of form, what it really gets to is at the core of it, you feel like you really messed up and you are fundamentally a mess-up.

OPRAH: *But that's an ego thing, isn't it?*

PEMA: That's the crux of ego. But if you just make friends with ego rather than try to obliterate it or call it bad. And making friends with it means to know it 100 percent completely. Don't reject it. Believe it or not, that's how you begin to become a more egoless person. Because the only reason we do this grasping and fixating and all of this on what you call ego is because we feel we have something to protect. We don't want to go to that place. We don't want to feel that way. If people can hold or embrace or allow their nervous system to handle the suffering, the uncomfortableness, the insecurity.

OPRAH: *The discontent.*

PEMA: The discontent. Then there is a chance of letting the evolution happen.

"*Forgiveness is giving
up the hope that the past
could be any different.*"
*It's accepting the past for
what it was and using this
moment and this time to
help yourself move forward.*

—Oprah

CHAPTER SIX

FORGIVENESS

For so many people searching for peace and purpose, the most debilitating source of pain has been the struggle to forgive.

Having experienced the trauma of childhood abuse and personal betrayals at different points of my life, I have great compassion for anyone facing what might seem like an insurmountable hurdle. The journey to release all grudges, to relinquish the quest for revenge, and to let go of the fantasy of what might have been is one of the most difficult spiritual challenges we'll ever face. But I promise you, it is also the most rewarding. Because the other side of forgiveness is freedom.

There was a time when I believed the act of forgiveness meant accepting the offender, and by doing so, condoning the act. I didn't understand that the true purpose of forgiveness is to stop allowing whatever that person did to affect how I live my life now.

I only began to see a different path for myself after an expert

on *The Oprah Winfrey Show*, Dr. Gerald G. Jampolsky, shared his definition:

"Forgiveness is giving up the hope that the past could be any different."

Those words gave me goose bumps! This was a transcendent moment for me, bigger than an *aha*. I loved this idea so much, I adopted it as my personal mantra.

Accepting this principle as spiritual law took me to the next level of living my own best life. And if you watch *Super Soul Sunday*, you know that I continue to share it regularly. In return, the life experiences shared with me on *Super Soul Sunday* have allowed me to go deeper and expand further into how forgiveness functions. My hope is that you, too, will use the wisdom in this chapter to excavate where you need to forgive.

When best-selling author and spiritual teacher Iyanla Vanzant joined me on the show, I told her that I keep the lesson in forgiveness she shared with me in a little book of quotes I've collected over the years:

"You can accept or reject the way you are treated by other people, but until you heal the wounds of your past, you will continue to bleed. You can bandage the bleeding with food, with alcohol, with drugs, with work, with cigarettes, with sex, but eventually, it will ooze through and stain your life. You must find the strength to open the wounds, stick your hands inside, pull out the core of the pain that is holding you in your past, the memories, and make peace with them."

This speaks so clearly to me. Pushing against the need to forgive is like spreading poison in your veins. Surrender to the hurt, loss, resentment, and disappointment. Accept the truth. It did happen and now it's done. Make a decision to meet the pain as it rises within you and allow it to pass right through. Give yourself permission to let go of the past and step out of your history, into the now.

Forgive, and set yourself free.

—*Oprah*

Everything you blame, you're stuck with. Bless it. Wish it well. Wish it its own freedom, and it will be very powerful in the way that it will not come back to you. If you don't forgive it, if you don't bless it, if you don't wish it well, the energy will just be magnetically drawn back to you because it's looking for resolution. All negative energy that we've inherited, it's there because it's looking for resolution.

—*Adyashanti*

MARK NEPO

We've talked before about paradox, which is held in any moment when more than one thing is true. Accountability and forgiveness form a paradox. On the one side, accountability is always true. You know, people are accountable for what they do to each other. And we do hurt each other, and sometimes we don't own that and that hurts even further. Yet every experience we have reveals to us a word in the language of our own wisdom, which only we can start to learn. And when we resist that, we can't understand our own experience, and then we can't understand each other.

WAYNE DYER

My father walked out on us. He just abandoned us. My mother had three boys under the age of four before she was twenty-three years old. It was the Great Depression. And I carried around deep anger and deep resentment and deep hatred. I dreamed every night—*rage* was a good word, because at night, I would wake up and I would be sweating. I tried to find him. I ended up in Biloxi, Mississippi, at his grave. I didn't even know he was dead up until just a few months earlier. And his body had been shipped there. And when I went to the grave and I stood there, I finally said, "From this moment on, I send you love. From this moment on, I will no longer have any resentment or hatred or bitterness toward you." I never dreamed about this man again. I feel his presence very, very frequently. From that moment on, I quit drinking. Alcohol was no longer a part of my life. I lost the weight, and I changed my diet around. The right people began to show up in my life. And it was all about forgiveness.

Pastor JOHN GRAY

PASTOR JOHN GRAY: On my dad's deathbed, I told him, "I forgive you for not being there, and I'm going to make your name good." Because I'm John W. Gray III. And I believe that I'm a continuation of his legacy. And I was the last person to see him alive. I sang hymns over his bed, prayed with him, told him I was going to make him proud. And so even now at forty-two, sometimes I look out the window hoping he's coming down the street.

OPRAH: *Wow.*

JOHN: And I'd seen him only four times.

OPRAH: *That is amazing*

JOHN: I just love him. And I didn't know him.

OPRAH: *How were you able to forgive him for not being there?*

JOHN: My connection to God helped me to deconstruct my dad's life backward. I had to look at his life through his death. My relationship to his mother, my grandmother, who was very stern, very closed off, unemotional.

OPRAH: *So you got to see who he was by deconstructing his life.*

JOHN: And so I had grace for him.

OPRAH: *Oh. Grace.*

JOHN: I was able to not be angry because I understood what it must have been like to live in that atmosphere every single day with a woman who you could never please. And if you failed, then, of course, you were shunned. And so to a large extent, I began to have more grace for my dad.

You will forgive because you love yourself so much that you don't want to keep hurting yourself for whatever happened. Whatever happened is done and cannot be changed. And we have to accept that and keep going with our life.

—*Don Miguel Ruiz*

TRACEY JACKSON

We spend so much time defending our mistakes, hiding from our mistakes, making excuses for our mistakes, and never just looking at 'em and going, "Whoa, this is me. This is me. This is my mistake. I'm gonna clean up my side of the street." And we do something that I call the emotional Sherpa. We carry around so much baggage of all the stuff we've done. And we carry it around, and it's heavy, and we unload it onto others, which is completely unfair. A mistake is our best teacher if you just take it and go, "I'm not a bad person. I made a mistake, and I've learned a lesson." And any day you learn a lesson is a great day.

SHAKA SENGHOR

OPRAH: *Forgiveness is. Complete that sentence. Forgiveness is …*

SHAKA SENGHOR: Freeing yourself from anger that's standing in the way of your growing as a human being.

OPRAH: *How are you able to forgive yourself?*

SHAKA: By stepping outside of myself and really seeing the little boy who was born with goodness. And that's been the hardest part of my journey, to forgive myself for the murder. I've been able to forgive myself for a lot of stuff, but that part has been hard.

OPRAH: *You wrote your victim, David, a letter. And what did you do that for? What did you want to say?*

SHAKA: I wanted to say that I'm sorry, that that night I made that decision. And I wanted to say it to myself, that I made that decision.

OPRAH: *He didn't make you make that decision.*

SHAKA: He didn't make me make that decision. I, myself, was responsible.

OPRAH: *Redemption is?*

SHAKA: Being given a second chance to prove who you are authentically. As humans, we're all capable of making a poor decision. But we're fully capable of moving beyond those decisions and doing something meaningful with our lives despite that—we don't have to be held hostage by it. And I think about that word often when I encounter obstacles. And all I ever wanted was a fair chance to just be a human. To me, that's what redemption represents: Just give me a fair chance to be a human.

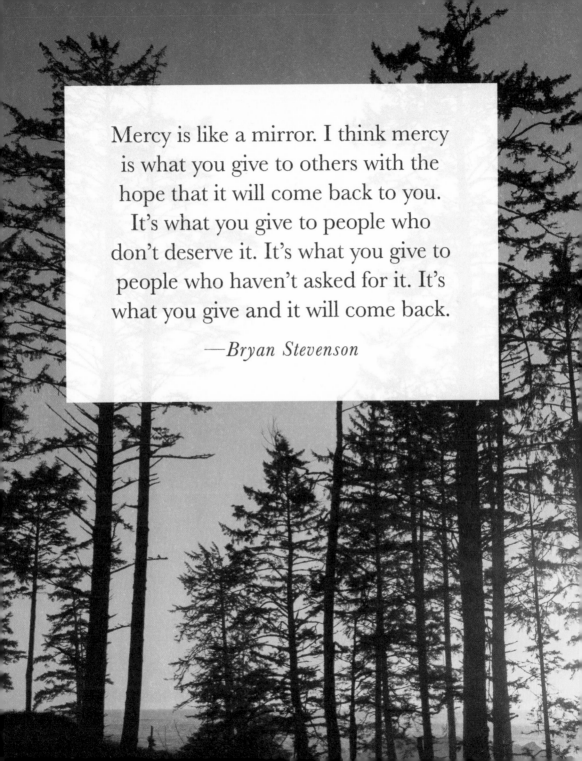

Mercy is like a mirror. I think mercy is what you give to others with the hope that it will come back to you. It's what you give to people who don't deserve it. It's what you give to people who haven't asked for it. It's what you give and it will come back.

—*Bryan Stevenson*

MICHAEL SINGER

OPRAH: *My prayer for the past couple of years, even before I ended* The Oprah Show, *was, "A closer walk with God." Now, I think when I was praying that prayer I thought that meant walking through the lilies of the field. There would be lots of roses going through the garden, you know? Because you think that's what it's going to be, and sometimes it's not.*

MICHAEL SINGER: "You must die to be reborn." It means you must be willing to let go of your personal self, of your psychological self, of the complaining voices.

OPRAH: *Your identity.*

MICHAEL: All that.

OPRAH: *Your image … all that.*

MICHAEL: Yes. In order to be who you are, you must be willing to let go of who you think you are. That's what's meant by "You must die to be reborn." And as you let that go, God will help pull it out, right? And so you use it spiritually and you will see that it will help you more than any meditation or anything else. You meditate so that you have the center so you can let go of what life is doing. The real growth is letting go.

There is not one experience, no matter how devastating, no matter how torturous it may appear to have been, there is nothing that's ever wasted. Everything that is happening to you is being drawn into your life as a means to help you evolve into who you were really meant to be here on Earth. It's not the thing that matters, it's what that thing opens within you.

—*Oprah*

CHAPTER SEVEN

BROKEN OPEN

One of my favorite questions to ask on *Super Soul Sunday* is, "What is the lesson that took you the longest to learn?"

The responses are always thoughtful, unique, and deeply personal.

My own answer to that question has taken a lifetime to learn.

I have struggled with my weight for much of my adult life. And I now realize I've been lying to myself about it for just as long. Lying is something I abhor. And lying to yourself is the worst.

In the deepest part of myself, I think I always knew that I was using food to repress my feelings. Any hint of discomfort or agitation that could lead to confrontation, rejection, or anyone being upset would cause me to eat. And after talking to so many people on *The Oprah Winfrey Show* and *Super Soul Sunday*, I knew my emotional eating stemmed from a childhood spent getting punished for expressing my feelings. After a few "whoopings," as they were called in my day, I learned quickly how to push my emotions down. I understood, even as a six-year-old, that my feelings would not be validated.

So even though I knew the root of my weight issues, I only recently discovered how to fix them.

As a spiritual seeker, I understand that this journey requires you to not only embrace all that is whole and good in your life but also to continually examine the long-buried wounds hidden beneath your carefully crafted surface.

This is what I mean when I say, "Turn your wounds into wisdom."

It turns out, when it comes to my issues with weight, I needed to take a bit of my own advice.

Despite the freedom I felt in forgiving those who hurt me in the past, it's taken me years (and many *Super Soul* conversations) to understand that another unresolved issue existed under the extra weight I was carrying.

I realize now that even though I have had the kind of career that brings with it an element of power, versions of my childhood abuser continually showed up in my life disguised in other forms. This person might have been wearing a skirt, or a different pair of pants, but the same relationship dynamic was there. I allowed abusers to cross boundaries rather than confronting them.

My childhood history of physical and sexual abuse conditioned me to be silent in overbearing and uncomfortable situations. I pushed those feelings down with food.

Years after I became known in the world, I found myself in my father's house with one of the men who had molested me. I couldn't fully explain it to myself at the time, but there I was in the kitchen making eggs for him. He told me he liked his eggs over easy, and I thought, *Oh my God, I'm standing here making eggs for this man, and I don't even know why I'm in the room.*

Looking back, this was a seminal moment for me. I reverted to the silence of my nine-year-old girl self, who thought that speaking up would cause me to be blamed. It has finally clicked that this type of compliant relationship has replayed over and over in both my personal and professional life. If I ever became upset about something, rather than speaking out, I reverted to the silence of that nine-year-old girl—just like I did years later by making those eggs for a man who had molested me.

I finally realized if I was ever going to establish a healthy relationship with my weight, the key was to confront whatever needed confrontation instead of suppressing and eating it.

Making that connection feels like a light bulb has finally been switched on. *Aha! Not only have I broken open, I've broken through!*

Shedding the weight now isn't about meeting goals on the scale or fitting into a dress. It means allowing myself to tell the truth and live in truth on every level, especially when I'm not happy about something. I've claimed my own freedom by telling people what I really feel at all times, even if it means the end of a relationship.

For anyone living with layers of shame, suppression, or secrecy, certain triggers may force you to confront all of those feelings you have kept at arm's length.

So many spiritual teachers have shared on *Super Soul Sunday* how our greatest epiphanies reveal themselves in times of deep turmoil and despair. Job loss, addiction, a breakup, the death of a loved one, illness—these are the types of struggles that can break us wide open. Best-selling author of *Eat Pray Love* and frequent *Super Soul Sunday* guest Elizabeth Gilbert calls these "bathroom floor moments." Others call them "dark nights of the soul."

Before you start looking outside yourself, asking, *Why me, why me, why me?*, understand that nothing is happening out of order with you. Your life is always speaking to you, just like my weight was constantly reminding me of what I thought I had resolved. When that reckoning comes for you, remember it's really your life trying to push you in another direction. It is opening the door to your next great journey. And know this for sure, no experience is wasted.

Challenges provide opportunities that force us to search for a new center of gravity. Don't resist. Resistance only causes more struggle. You can't win if you're fighting the truth. Instead, persist in finding and letting it break you open.

—Oprah

ELIZABETH LESSER

You can either break down and stay broken down and eventually shut down, or you can break open. It's a decision you make. It's a commitment. *I am going through a very hard time. I'm not going to waste this precious experience, this opportunity to become the best me.*

Through the experience of getting divorced and becoming a single mother, I lost everything—my financial security, my self-image, my support, my home. Everything changed for me. In the depth of that loss, I found out who I really was. I began to trust who I was. I began to find a genuine me that could withstand anything. And if we fight those times and fight the bud opening, we live half of a life. But when we open into our brokenness, that's when we blossom.

Sometimes when we wake up
to spirituality, and you've seen it
everywhere, the you-know-what hits the
fan. And everything falls apart. Those
are the moments when we get to work.
Those are not the moments when we
drink. Those are not the moments when
we go back to the addiction. Those
are the moments when we get to work.
Because those moments are showing
up to help you show up. Pay attention
to the assignments that are coming to
you, and show up for them! Everything
comes up so it can be healed.

—*Gabrielle Bernstein*

Success doesn't teach you anything. I'm going to say up to the age of thirty, you need some successes to create your ego structure. But it's an arbitrary number. After thirty, everything I've learned has been from humiliation, sin, failure, rejection, betrayal. That's when my soul expands. Now, I don't like it. And I don't know it till afterward, too. You know, you want to get rid of it. But then two days later, in the surrendering, the accepting, the seeing, I realize I'm larger and larger.

—*Father Richard Rohr*

ALI MACGRAW

OPRAH: *I think being spiritual is about coming into who you really are, what you're really meant to be. That's what the path looks like for me. When you turned sixty-five, was that a scary moment? Was it a moment of reckoning?*

ALI MACGRAW: You know what I did? It's so funny. I keep a journal only when I travel, and I went to this place that a friend owns in a little corner of Mexico, and I brought a book and brilliantly colored double-ended pens. And I locked myself in my room and I wrote the today-I'm-sixty-five thing. And I wrote stuff like, *Am I ever gonna have sex again?* in red. Or *Do I have to do something about the third chin?* in a hideous electric green. So I couldn't hide behind the kind of truths you talk about with your best girlfriend. I told myself some of the vanity scares. And I wrote and I cried and

I wrote and I cried, and then I got so bored with it. It was like two days of drinking tea and writing my true scary stuff and a lot of other things.

OPRAH: *Were you scared not to be called pretty anymore?*

ALI: I was scared about all the things that we're taught we should start getting scared about. And I wrote them, and then I went, *Okay, that's it.* And I felt like it's time—you know, *I've got that one down. Now let's go on and live.* It was a very jubilant day.

OPRAH: *So it was an exorcism of sorts?*

ALI: It was a total exorcism.

SARAH BAN BREATHNACH

OPRAH: *Was it a surprise to you, the way the world responded to your book* Simple Abundance?

SARAH BAN BREATHNACH: Oh, yes.

OPRAH: *Did you kind of lose your mind?*

SARAH: I tried very hard not to. One minute I was doing the car pool and changing the cat litter and writing about gratitude and being told that no lifestyle book based on gratitude is ever going to catch fire. And then the next minute, I was asked to do it. Yes, in a word, it blew my mind.

OPRAH: *I had been a person who practiced gratitude, and what* Simple Abundance *did for me is to ritualize, to bring into my life on a daily basis, the experience of practicing gratitude. But it's really difficult when not just money but real wealth hits and you're not pre-pared for it. When it comes, you have to really be ready for it. Were you ready?*

SARAH: No, I was not. And you know, that was such a completely head-turning, heart-turning flip-out. So I tried my hardest, you know.

OPRAH: *So you quickly rose to that lifestyle.*

SARAH: Yes.

OPRAH: *Did you know what you could afford and couldn't afford at that time?*

SARAH: No. I also didn't know, as I took on staff, how much that was costing.

OPRAH: *You had nine assistants?*

SARAH: I had nine assistants.

OPRAH: *Nine assistants, their salaries, health insurance, their travel …*

SARAH: Their mortgages. I made every money mistake a woman could have, personally and in business.

OPRAH: *Why did you make those mistakes?*

SARAH: I really thought it would continue because I was putting out the best that I could do.

OPRAH: *You were like a rock star with a hit album, who thinks,* I will just contin-ue to make the hits and the hits will keep on coming and I'll go on tour and it'll be here forever.

SARAH: Right.

OPRAH: *After* Simple Abundance *became a phenomenon, you returned to England and fell in love. It would be your third marriage, and it turned out it wasn't the love story you'd hoped.*

SARAH: We were all right for the first couple of years, although he told me that I was no good with money, despite the fact that I made the money.

OPRAH: *And you believed that—because there was a part of you that would have to—the only way you could accept it is if there was a part of you that believed it was true. So how could you allow yourself to be berated for money that you had earned?*

SARAH: You know, the first time it happens, you think that's a little out of line.

OPRAH: *I call those the whispers—first time is always,* Hmm, that's odd.

SARAH: That's strange.

OPRAH: *He should not be talking to me that way.*

SARAH: Right. And I also wanted his approval, but then you start to get beaten down, and so the next question is, why'd you stay?

The first two years, you know, had been all right. I thought that it wasn't that bad.

OPRAH: *I love the way you say, "It wasn't that bad." You who wrote* Simple Abundance, *you're willing to now live with "wasn't that bad"? I think all of us make compromises. I remember in my twenties, being in a relationship with someone who didn't hit me, and that was my limit, because I wouldn't allow myself to be hit, but I would allow myself to be demeaned in other ways. I figured that out in my twenties, and I think that's really the real lesson for everybody, that even though you had all of the trappings of success and you looked like it and you walked like it, the click of your Manolo Blahniks on the pavement said, "I am successful," that still somewhere inside you must have not felt that in an authentic, pure way in order to put up with somebody berating you.*

SARAH: I'll accept that, but you get battered down and you become very, very vulnerable.

OPRAH: *Are you saying that you stayed because you felt dependent upon him at that time? Or you felt that you were tied to him?*

SARAH: No, by the time that it happened around our second anniversary, he really changed his behavior toward me, and at some point, I said, "Why are you treating me so mean? What's happened?" And he said, "Because all the money's gone." I thought that couldn't possibly be true, but it was true.

OPRAH: *What disturbed you the most—the fact that all the money was gone or the fact that you didn't matter as much because all the money was gone?*

SARAH: Oh, the fact that I didn't matter. It was like, "What?"

OPRAH: *"So you were only here because I had the money?" That was the realization for you?*

SARAH: That was, and I was ashamed, and then the very things that he was saying I started to believe. You know, if somebody hits you, you know to get out …

OPRAH: *That's it! "You're not going to hit me!"*

SARAH: But when it's these angry, vicious things that are said … And I didn't want to admit that I had made a disastrous mistake.

OPRAH: *I just want to say this: that it*

always, always, always—and you know this—it's always about you. Nobody can speak to you in a way that demeans your spirit unless you are willing to be demeaned or feel that you deserve that in some way. Would you agree with that?

SARAH: Yes, I would. I was betraying myself on many levels, but then, I mean, the horror story has a happy ending in that I left.

OPRAH: *What gave you the courage to get up and leave?*

SARAH: My daughter came over. She was worried about me, and she said, "Mom, what's going on?" She said, "He's sucking the life out of you. He's not making you happy." And I said, "You're right." And then I said, "I don't know how to help myself." She said, "Mom, you've helped millions of women. I'll help you help yourself." I said, "I don't know; I don't know where to begin." She said, "We'll begin."

OPRAH: *So you ended up on your sister's doorstep with your cat. And one suitcase.*

SARAH: And divorce proceedings starting.

OPRAH: *You went from* Simple Abundance *to real* abundance, *to your sister's doorstep. And that's how your book* Peace and Plenty *came to be. Was writing that good for you?*

SARAH: Yes. I was writing for my life. I was not writing to make a hit; this was my life on the page. Understanding money, seeing how money, my mistakes with money, how that had influenced all my decisions.

OPRAH: *Have you reached a place of serenity for yourself?*

SARAH: Some days are more authentic than others. Some days are more financially serene.

OPRAH: *I loved your chapter that you did on "Tomorrow Is Another Day." Because it is. You can get up and you have a chance—you know that famous Scarlett O'Hara line, "Tomorrow is another day." The real truth is, mistakes are Life's way of pointing you in another direction to say, "Tomorrow is another day, Scarlett." We can try it again.*

SARAH: Yes, I really felt that when the car pulled out of the driveway in England. Even though I was leaving everything behind, didn't know what would happen, I really felt that "Whew." That heaven went, "Whew, she got it. She got it."

CAROLINE MYSS

I need you to be fully present and appreciate all that is in your life right now. No matter where it is. You are in the depths of despair, and still I need to say to you, you had your life focused on something that didn't belong to you and a path that didn't belong to you. Yes, you did, or you wouldn't be here. You locked in on something that did not belong to you. Someone that didn't belong to you. You didn't let go of a yesterday that didn't belong to you. You hung on to a rage that did belong to you and you wouldn't let it go. You lost track of being here, and that is true, or this is what you did.

One of those things happened, and you said, "It shouldn't have happened to me." I promise you that happened. When someone finally said, "It's not my life. I don't know how I lost my purpose." No, you didn't. You did not lose your purpose. What you lost was the sense that you thought certain things shouldn't happen to you and they did. As if you were excluded from the ordinary everyday things of life and you can't get over it. People hold the idea of being ordinary in absolute contempt. "Please, God, make me anything, but not ordinary." And because they do that, they feel like they should be protected from ordinary things. So when something happens like an illness, poverty, any kind of catastrophe, they think, *I can't believe this happened to me.*

LLEWELLYN VAUGHAN-LEE

OPRAH: *You talk about the journey to spirituality being painful.*

LLEWELLYN VAUGHAN-LEE: Yes, it is painful. One has to learn humility. You have to learn patience. You have to learn that it isn't about you. And those are all painful lessons. We don't learn them so easily as human beings. We want it to be easy, but it isn't.

OPRAH: *Why must it be so painful?*

LLEWELLYN: Because the heart has to break open. Most people are so closed, they are so contracted. It's all about me, me, me.

OPRAH: *And that's what you mean by the crucifixion of the ego?*

LLEWELLYN: Crucifixion, yes. Then the heart breaks, and God says, "I am with those whose hearts are broken for My sake."

OPRAH: *So, by the crucifixion of the ego, you mean the heart has to break. You have to get taken out of the sense that everything that's happening is about you?*

LLEWELLYN: There you go. That's right.

OPRAH: *And so then you begin to live your life in alignment with the Beloved. In alignment with God; asking God constantly in a constant state of how can I serve?*

LLEWELLYN: Yes.

OPRAH: *But I would say, when you are in alignment and you are in service to what God wants you to do, it's also the most exhilarating, the most stimulating—really, I'm going to cry—and the most beautiful.*

LLEWELLYN: Yes, it is. You want nothing more ... just to be in service for the rest of your life.

MICHAEL BERNARD
BECKWITH

When circumstances and situations are pressing in upon us, the only way we can overcome them is to go within. To actually begin to ask very empowering questions with the awareness that this Universal Presence and its law will answer any question that you ask. So if you're in a situation that is pressing on you and you ask, "What's trying to emerge in my life? What is my gift to share? What is my purpose? Why am I here on the planet?" Not just "How can I pay my rent?" Not just "How can I stop the pain?" You ask empowering questions. The Universe will answer these questions in a language and in a way that you can understand. There will be inter-prompting, there will be intuitive hits, nudges, signs, symbols, dreams. It'll come in the language of the individual's soul and heart. The difficulty is that when people are in tough situations, they ask disempowering questions. They say, "What's wrong? Who's

to blame? Why me?" Those are the disempowering questions. So the Universe will answer those, too. It will pull on the database of human experience and say you were born on the wrong side of the tracks or you were born on the right side of the tracks or this happened or that happened. It will give you a bevy of excuses. But if you ask an empowering question, you'll get an answer to rise above the muck. So it's all about the question, the sincerity of the question, and then the ability and the willingness to really listen, to really be available. That's where the juice is. Whether an individual is in prison, whether an individual is imprisoned by circumstance, in prison in their own mind about an event that happened in their past— it doesn't matter. Once you ask with sincerity, the Universe will answer. That's the way it operates. And our way is love, kindness, compassion, and service.

ELIZABETH GILBERT

OPRAH: *Tell us about that moment of despair, where you're in the bathroom.*

ELIZABETH GILBERT: Okay, I'm not somebody who really grew up praying. We went to a very conservative Protestant church, where you didn't really pray, you know? So I just started praying, I had this … I thought, *Oh … I've heard of this,* right? *When people are in despair and they're sobbing and sometimes they pray, so let me give that a shot,* you know. And I just started speaking directly. I had no experience how to do it, but I just said to God, "I need Your help. I don't know what to do. Please tell me what to do." And the decision I was struggling with was, do I stay in this marriage, do I leave this marriage? And I just kept saying over and over again, "Tell me what to do. Tell me what to do. Tell me what to do." And I kept waiting for the big sort of Charlton Heston answer—you know, "Yes, stay." "No, go." But that's not how it works.

And what happened was that, all of a sudden, I fell into this pocket of stillness unlike anything I had ever felt in my life. This divine, quiet envelope of peace. And I heard this voice, that was my own voice, but not, in my head, and it said very clearly, "Go back to bed, Liz." And that was the answer God gave me that night, which was "You don't need to know tonight, on a Tuesday at four o'clock in the morning what to do, because you don't know and you won't know until you do know. But in the meantime, you need to sleep, because you need your rest and you need your strength. Go back to bed; I'll keep the watch, we'll try it again tomorrow." And every night came, "Go back to bed; we're getting there. When you know, you'll do it. You'll do the change."

GLENNON DOYLE

I felt split in two my entire life. There is the part of me on the outside that's saying the things that I'm supposed to say, like, "I'm fine. I'm fine. I'm fine. Everything's good. Marriage? It's like Disney. Parenting? Fulfilled." And then there's the part on the inside of me that's scared and lonely and confused a lot. And what I really think is that we are all truth tellers. I think we were just made to tell the truth. And it's very hard for the world to hear the truth from a woman. It's easier for the world to hear the truth from a man. But since negative emotions are less acceptable from a woman, we end up sometimes telling our truth in different ways than words. Dangerous ways. Like, this was the food for me, the booze for me. I think we tell the truth with something.

Everybody tells the truth with something. Whether they say, "I'm not fine with a credit card," or they say, "I'm not fine with overeating," or they say, "I'm not fine with booze or sex or unkindness," or whatever it is. Which is why it's so powerful when you can integrate those two selves and tell the truth of the story of what's going on inside with your words.

MICHAEL SINGER

If your body starts to hurt, you don't say, "Shut up." You say, "Well, I wonder what's wrong. It's trying to talk to me." Likewise the pain you feel in your heart is your heart telling you something's wrong. You want to get it out, how do you get it out? You relax and it will work itself out. That is my experience. You relax and don't touch; it will come up and push its own way out. It's almost as if your heart doesn't want that inside. And when you do that, you will start to feel something open up inside of you, I guarantee you. You can call it spirit, call it whatever you want, you will start to feel a strength, a power, behind you. Not in front of you, where the thorns are—behind you where you've been leaning back into.

IYANLA VANZANT

There are four primal fears.

Number one, the fear of losing someone's love or having your love rejected. The human mind just can't even handle that.

The fear of being powerless or helpless and, therefore, you're not safe in your being. So the fear of being unsafe.

The third fear is really the number-one human addiction. The number-one human addiction is not chocolate. It's control. So that third fear is the fear of losing control. Control of yourself. Control of others. Control of what will happen, how it will happen, when it will happen sends the human ego into total meltdown.

And then the fourth fear is just not being seen as valuable, worthy, necessary.

Anger is really the manifestation of one of those fears. That your love is being rejected or that it's going to be taken away. That you're going to be seen as helpless, hopeless, therefore, vulnerable. And you know the ego can't stand vulnerability. So in order not to be vulnerable, you want to maintain control. When you can't control how somebody's doing what they're doing, there's a fear there. And that takes us into anger.

Now, here's the thing about anger that I hope everyone can get. You're never angry for the reason you think you are. We're not born with it. So something happened and you had that helpless, hopeless, vulnerable, powerless lack of control response and that made an impression. The experience made the imprint, and then on the soul there's an impression. And anytime anything that looks like, sounds like, smells like is related to that first impression, raises those feelings up in you, the anger is stirred up. So you think you're angry because Boo-Boo left you. No. That is really not the origin. Boo-Boo was the trigger. Boo-Boo is just coming into your life to remind you that there's something down there you need to handle.

Right beneath the anger there is a well of hurt. And we stay at the anger because it gives us control, because we are afraid to go into the hurt. Because right beneath the hurt is the love.

This is what I want you to do. I want you to drop your hands to your sides. I also want you to disconnect your brain. That means close your eyes. Take a breath. It won't kill you. And invite the hurt forward. Just invite it forward. Invite it forward. You've got to get into the true feeling. You've got to go there. Drop to the hurt.

Dr. SHEFALI TSABARY

With every conflict with your child, with every argument, with every eye roll that your child engages in, you have an opportunity to either step into your egoic control and power and dominance and hierarchy, or you have a chance to look within. Ask, *What in me is being triggered? Why am I reacting with this confused helplessness? This desire to seek control?* And turn the mirror inward. Ask, *What about me is my child triggering right now? What about me? What about my childhood? What about my unmothered self is my child reflecting back?*

PEMA CHÖDRÖN

Self-improvement means that I'm going to be different than I am now. But, if the view changes instead to the belief that there's nothing wrong here, I haven't done anything wrong, but there are things obstructing me from fully feeling self-improved, well, then let's just look at those things and know them completely and utterly.

Let's know our rage, let's know our fear, let's know our resentment. And by knowing it, listening to what you say about yourself and letting some of that negative self-talk go, you know? Then the fundamental thing is there. It's like the sun is always shining, but there are clouds obstructing it.

CHERYL STRAYED

OPRAH: *If you had to sum it up, what did the trail teach you?*

CHERYL STRAYED: Acceptance. Accept the fact of the hour. The fact of the mile. The fact of the summer. The facts of my life. And over and over again, I found that if I could do that, everything else sort of gave way. And it led me into the next step, the next thing that was going to reveal itself. And I think that is such a powerful and important thing.

We all suffer. We all have heartbreak. We all have difficult things, and you know, that's part of life. And that was really a profound thing for me to accept and to come to grips with. And that journey that summer taught me a really grand sense of humility that you have to keep walking in ways both physical or literal and metaphorical.

What you can do in any situation, no matter what the challenge is, you can always go to your state of being. And how do you go to your state of being? You stop. No matter what the challenge is, you stop. You take a few deep breaths. You smile everywhere in your body. You observe what is happening in your body, in your mind, and then you proceed with loving-kindness and compassion. Stop. S, stop. T, take three deep breaths. O, observe. P, proceed with kindness and joy and love. That's the state of being. It's the highest form of human intelligence.

—*Deepak Chopra*

ADYASHANTI

We're not taught that difficulty can have a profound and meaningful, transformative effect on us. You know, we might be taught that in a way someone might say that. But what do I do? What do I do when I'm suffering? What do I do when I feel overwhelmed? How do I work with the minutiae of my experience so that it's transformative and not just another episode of suffering in a lifetime of suffering?

The first thing is, you have to be unconditionally open to it. And take responsibility. *How have I gotten myself right here? Am I willing to see how I got myself here?*

If somebody else was fully to blame for my current state, whatever that is?

Then that's it. I'm done. I have no hope. If they're the real blame, I can't go back and change anything that's ever happened. I'm stuck. That's hopeless.

But when we realize that may have affected how I experience this moment, there's a link.

And there's usually things about it that we don't want to own up to. And it's difficult, and once you start, you start to realize it's very

liberating. Because the keys to your happiness are no longer in somebody else's pocket from the past. They're in yours. And that's … that's empowering.

And I'm talking about people I've seen do this who have horrendously difficult pasts, extraordinarily traumatic, violent pasts, who can really come to see *How am I sustaining that trauma? How am I traumatizing myself? How am I continuing it? Not in the sense of being to blame for it. But since the past isn't here now, how is it that I'm keeping it alive? What are the dynamics? What's actually happening?*

As a human being, I have a history. But as my essence, I realized I have no history. Eternity knows no history. Eternity is the eternal presence. So when you or I become completely present—because eternity is always right now, when we're completely present with anything—all of a sudden at that moment, for how long it lasts, there's no yesterday, there's no ten years ago. There's not even a minute ago. It's all gone. All it knows is this instance.

The most fundamental lesson that you can take away from Super Soul Sunday *is gratitude. Gratitude is its own energy field. When you acknowledge and are grateful for whatever you have, it allows more to be drawn to you and changes the way you experience life. Grace is transformative. The more grateful you are, the more grace mirrors the gratitude that you have.*

—*Oprah*

CHAPTER EIGHT

GRACE AND GRATITUDE

It's been twenty years since I first read Sarah Ban Breathnach's *Simple Abundance* **and started keeping a gratitude journal.**

Looking back, I believe it was the one of the most important things I've done.

I've been keeping diaries since I was fifteen years old, but before I began focusing on gratitude, they were always filled with bad poetry and "woe is me" worries about my weight, men, and what other people thought about me.

I can't tell you how much my life changed when I started writing down five things I was grateful for each day. It sounds simple, but when you go through the day staying conscious about what you will put on your gratitude list, it completely shifts the lens through which you see the world.

Without even realizing it, gratitude opens a fresh new channel within you, a place where the spiritual dimension of your life can flow. As your true self grows in the space of gratefulness, you can't help but feel more alive and receptive to the beauty that surrounds you. And because I believe what we focus on expands, the more we celebrate gratitude, the more blessings come into our lives.

Imagine all of this goodness appearing simply by staying still long enough to notice the morning, the sun, a perfect rose, or someone taking the time to hold the door for you.

I know it's not easy to be grateful all the time, but I've learned that it's when you feel the least thankful that you are most in need of what gratitude can give you: perspective.

It was my soul sister, mother figure, mentor, and friend Dr. Maya Angelou who taught me what she believed to be the true purpose of giving thanks. After I called her years ago, upset and in tears over what I thought someone had done to me, she stopped me mid-sob and said, "Stop your crying right now and say thank you."

I was confused and asked, "Why?"

"Because," she said in that deep, wise Maya Angelou voice, "you know God put a rainbow in every cloud. The rainbow is coming. Say thank you even though you can't see the rainbow. It's already there."

So many of the great teachers who've joined me on *Super Soul Sunday* have helped me see how the practice of gratitude can elevate your life to a state of grace. Their lessons on the following pages will help you see how grace is a natural extension of the gratitude you feel in your own life.

Today, I give thanks for the breath in my lungs, my body that has carried me to every corner of this magnificent Earth, and my connection to the source of *All* things—*All* knowing, *All* being, *All.*

As the German mystic Meister Eckhart once said so eloquently: *If the only prayer you say in your entire life is thank you, that will be enough.*

—*Oprah*

MARK NEPO

I was just writing the other day about being grateful, thanking God that my experiences have hollowed me out like a hollow bone. But I was never thankful while I was being hollowed out. And I think that's very human. When I have experienced difficult things with family or friends or in life situations, it's very hard. I certainly wasn't thankful to the pain in my stomach when I was recently ill. I didn't want it to be there. But trying to hold the larger view at the same time is where gratitude lives.

So let me give you an image. If you're at sea and you're in a raft and the swells of the sea are huge, when you are lifted to the top of a wave, you can see for eternity. When you come down into the belly of a wave, you can't see anything. The kind of gratitude we're talking about is not to deny the fact that you're in the belly of a wave and that wave might crash on you, but to never lose sight of the horizon even though in this moment you're not seeing it.

TONY ROBBINS

TONY ROBBINS: It takes high energy to make change. So when you're not suffering, when you're in a high state of love or creativity or gratitude or passion, in those states, you get the solution. I made this decision for myself, and this is just in the last year, Oprah. It's changed my life so much. I've always had a beautiful life. I've always been so grateful. Even in the tough times, I'm grateful. But I decided if I can't find ecstasy in this moment, whatever this moment is—having lunch, talking with you, walking through the forest, whatever it is—if I can't find ecstasy in this moment, then helping more people, changing more lives, building more businesses, none of that is going to make me happier. So my goal is to find that ecstasy. When you're suffering, it's hard to jump to ecstasy. So the first step I go to is appreciation.

OPRAH: *This moment, right here, now.*

TONY: Anything. The wind. The look in your eye. Something that I can appreciate. Because the minute you appreciate, you get out of your own self. You stop obsessing. It's like I always tell people, most of your suffering comes from expectation. Right? Trade your expectation for appreciation. Your whole life changes in that moment. Suffering ends in that moment. But, see, most people have a blueprint of how they think life's supposed to be, and when life matches the blueprint, I always say to people, "Tell me something you're happy about."

And they'll say, "Well, I'm not happy about much."

"Well, tell me one thing," and they'll go, "Well, I'm happy about my children," or "I'm happy about my relationship with God."

And so I'll say, "Why?"

And they'll say, "Well, because my children are the way I want them to be."

When life matches your blueprint, you're happy. When life doesn't match your blueprint, you have pain. When life doesn't match your blueprint, but you feel helpless to change it—that's when you suffer. That's when it's the dark night of the soul. That's when people feel like things can't happen. And the delusion is, it's just the mind taking over. When that happens, you have to blame someone, which is what most people do. They blame the environment or they blame someone else or they blame themselves. Blame doesn't change anything. Your other choices are change your friggin' life. Do something. Or change your blueprint.

RAM DASS

OPRAH: *In the period after your stroke did you ever feel sorry for yourself?*

RAM DASS: No. It just was a new stage of life.

OPRAH: *Did you come to understand what being spiritual meant in a different way with the stroke?*

RAM DASS: Yes. Suffering is grace. Not the stroke itself, but spiritual life is in the moment. In the moment is where you see God—not in the past, not in the future. Past and future are thoughts, just thoughts. It is just this moment.

OPRAH: *This is the moment where God lives. Right there in the stillness, right there in the still.*

RAM DASS: That's it, in the moment is where God lives—beautiful.

I love this Latin term *amor fati*—"love of fate." Instead of bemoaning your fate—and sometimes our fates are terrible—we love our fate. *Amor fati.* It's a way of being grateful. I'm going to love what happened to me because I trust it's here to remove a veil. I'm going to search for what's happening to me in this time so I can take away yet another misconception.

—*Elizabeth Lesser*

It's important to understand what grace feels like. It's where you feel, all of a sudden, overwhelmed by God's goodness. And you didn't deserve it. You didn't merit it. God just gave it to you because God loves you. That's grace. To the degree that we follow grace instead of trying to get out ahead of it and explain everything, grace will lead us to the reconciliation point. Reconciling our minds and our hearts, our souls and our intellects, our doctrine and our spirituality. The reconciliation point is there if we will follow grace.

—*Reverend Ed Bacon*

PAUL WILLIAMS *and* TRACEY JACKSON

TRACEY JACKSON: If you have gratitude, you don't have room for fear. And that was one of the biggest things—that fear holds us back so much. Fear is what causes so much of our bad behavior and our poor choices. And gratitude can't live with fear in the same way that love can't live with fear. So if you're grateful, you move to that place of love. And trust is soul, right? Trust is God.

PAUL WILLIAMS: Trust is the Big Amigo.

TRACEY: Trust is knowing that there's a power greater than yourself at work here. And trusting it will all work out.

PAUL: Yes. I'm grateful for everything that has ever happened in my life, the good and the bad. And you roll it into your life. If you're in a car wreck, you're grateful that nobody was hurt. If they're hurt, grateful that they didn't die. If they die, you're grateful for the chance you had to know them. You know, it's an expandable gratitude. One size fits all. Put it in your heart and use it.

Begin to notice what you have in your life that you are grateful for and when you look at life through the lens of gratitude, you don't see as many obstacles or hindrances. You see potential, you see possibilities. Then you become an open vehicle for more inspiration, more wisdom, more guidance, coming from the spiritual part of your being.

—*Michael Bernard Beckwith*

GENEEN ROTH

GENEEN ROTH: You're feeding your body. And for a long time, I didn't get that. I was eating for comfort, because I was sad because I was lonely, because I was grieving, because I was ashamed, because I felt unloved. But I didn't quite get that the food going in the mouth was about loneliness or comfort or sweetness or because I felt empty. I didn't think to have gratitude for having a body at all. Just sheer old, these arms and these legs and this heart and this liver have schlepped me, have taken me from place to place for so many years. And what have I done to it? I have basically just said, "I'm lonely. Here. Eat this." There wasn't appreciation. It wasn't "Thank you, body."

OPRAH: *I think about that a lot, certainly the more mature you get and thoughtful about yourself and your life. Like,* Wow, my heart has been pumping for sixty-two years. Wow! *And when you go to the doctor, I say, "Wow, you beautiful heart you. Pump on, girl." Yes. That's pretty amazing.*

GENEEN: It is amazing, and we don't consider it.

OPRAH: *Wherever you are in your life right now, your heart has been doing that.*

GENEEN: Without you asking.

OPRAH: *Thousands of times a day without you asking.*

CHERYL STRAYED

OPRAH: *Do you think that every person has that truth within them to speak, whether they can write it or not?*

CHERYL STRAYED: I do. I mean, obviously, you know, the work I do is as a writer. But the life I have is as a human. I think that every time you find that strength to show your truest self, you risk showing that self that makes you feel a little uncomfortable. A little like you found out you might be the weird one after all.

OPRAH: *Well, not just risk. To be brave enough to break your own heart. Which is your quote.*

CHERYL: That's right. Being brave enough to risk intimacy, to risk rejection, to risk failure. And all of the best things come when you do that.

OPRAH: *Because when you risk all of those things, you are really daring to be more human.*

CHERYL: You are. And sometimes you learn things the hard way and you never forget it, do you? And so being brave enough to break your own heart is about being brave enough to make the decisions that end up being really right for you. And also brave enough to sometimes make a decision that wasn't the best one in the end. But you learn from it. And life goes on. Hard times will come. But you know what else will always come? A sunrise and a sunset. And so it's up to you. You want to be there for it? Be there for it. It's about perspective and gratitude. And those two things are so key to a happy life.

CAROLINE MYSS

Do you ever have that in an argument with someone where you get so fired up and you think, *Ooh, I could just say this*? And all of a sudden, a voice says, "You sure you want to do that? Because it's a game changer … if you say that." That's grace.

The grace that comes in and says, "You can never take it back." The voice that comes in and says, "I'm going to prevent you from doing something really ruinous right now." That's grace. Here's grace. Grace is the kind of thing that comes in and says, "You'll be all right," and goes away. Grace is the kind of thing that says, "Put your hand on that person just for a minute." And you could feel an energy go through you and an energy calm them down. And it doesn't give you an explanation. When you are flushed with worry and you think, *Am I going to be all right?* And then you suddenly know, "Yes. Yes, you are." Grace is a power that comes in and transforms a moment to something better.

GRETCHEN RUBIN

OPRAH: *Do you think that being happier made you a more soulful, connected spiritual person?*

GRETCHEN RUBIN: One hundred percent. I was the least mindful person on the planet. And working on it like this really helped me connect to a more spiritual way of living.

OPRAH: *It seems like also living a life that allows you to be better than before, living a life where happiness and mindfulness is at the core of your center, it would bring you to a greater sense of awareness and fulfillment and gratitude. Like you would live in a space of gratitude.*

GRETCHEN: Absolutely. The sense of thankfulness, appreciating the grandeur of everyday life, just the ordinary day, and really taking the time to take it in is absolutely crucial. And then when you have that thankfulness, so many other negative emotions get washed away—resentment, anger, grievances, and grudges—because you're just so thankful for what you have. Also, it's better with a sense of humor. It helps me keep my sense of humor, because it helps me keep my sense of perspective.

SHAWN ACHOR

It's been found that if you wake up every morning and practice saying three things you are grateful for—they have to be new each day—by doing this for twenty-one days, even people who were testing as the low-level pessimist on average were now testing as low-level optimist. Now, that doesn't sound that huge, but here's the amazing thing. We can do this with eighty-four-year-old men with genes for pessimism. Not that all eighty-four-year-old men are pessimists, but we found some that were. And if you do this for twenty-one days, what we find is that even if you've practiced pessimism for eight decades of your life, even if you were born with genes for pessimism, when people practiced these, I would never guess before this research that literally two minutes could trump your genes and your environment. They sound like tips or tricks, but they're actually the building blocks of how human beings can change.

MARIE FORLEO

Many of us think that in order to find our passion, we have to look outside of ourselves. But I've learned that the secret, ironically, to finding your passion is to start bringing passion to everything you do. And I do mean everything. So no matter what task is in front of you, bring as much enthusiasm and energy to it as you possibly can. Whether you're making the bed, brushing your teeth, or cleaning the cat box, do it like you really want to do it. This one habit can change everything, because we humans are creatures of habit. You can't be complainy and miserable ninety percent of your day and expect to feel passionate the other ten percent. The willingness to take responsibility for your experience on a moment-to-moment basis is what we're missing. Most of us don't realize that passion is an inside job. It's a muscle that gets stronger the more you use it.

RUSSELL SIMMONS

Well, I think the stuff really teaches you, and you can learn it. People who are really rich have big struggles because they keep wanting more and more. And people who are really poor are told they need more, and so that causes the same kind of suffering. People in the middle ground sometimes—I think the research says they're usually happier because they kind of let go of it, you know.

And they never really associate their life with the stuff or the lack of stuff. But it's a comfortable seat. Right? What we want in life is a comfortable seat. And that's what they mean when they say operate from abundance or, you know, this idea of being awake and happy can only happen in the present moment.

LYNNE TWIST

OPRAH: *You say that if we explore our relationship with money, we can have this as a spiritual practice that leads to wholeness and fullness in every other area of our life. But when you say, "Everyone, let's explore your relationship with money," people start with what they don't have, I think.*

LYNNE TWIST: Yes. They start with "Give me more."

OPRAH: *What would bring me great joy is to know that after our conversation today, people would take the question "What is my relationship with money?" seriously and look at that. What are the questions one needs to ask oneself?*

LYNNE: Well, one needs to look at *What bounty and blessings have I received from the Universe that I want to acknowledge and celebrate? What do I want to celebrate about today? What happened today that I can celebrate, that I can be grateful for?* rather than waking up in the morning with *I didn't get enough sleep*, and going to bed at night with *I didn't get enough done*, which is bookending your day with scarcity.

OPRAH: *Yes. I think this is interesting for us to think about how many times a day that tape plays of "not enough." Not just in money. How many times a "not enough" shows up.*

LYNNE: But what if we woke up in the morning and were so grateful for the sweet territory of silence and sleep?

OPRAH: *Oh, I love that. Hold on a moment. "The sweet territory of silence and sleep." Oh, I like that. Go ahead.*

LYNNE: And you can wake up that way. You can actually tell yourself to do that. The mind is very obedient. Even if it's just four hours. The sweet territory of silence and sleep. And be grateful for that. And then at the end of the day, rather than looking at what didn't get done that's going to dribble over into tomorrow, which is where we mostly end up each day—to look at what I accomplished today. What I celebrate today. Every day is such a blessing. I have a wonderful teacher now, Brother David Steindl-Rast.

He's a fantastic Benedictine monk, and he's the icon of gratefulness. And he says that gratefulness is the experience of the great fullness of life. And when you're in the "great full" of any things of life, the bowl of life is so full, it's almost overflowing, but not quite. Not yet dribbling over the edges. And you're one with God, one with the Universe, and there is no other when you stand in and live in the great fullness of life. And that great fullness is so powerful that it overflows into a fountain in the bowl of life. And that puts you in this other branch of gratitude he calls Thanksgiving. And when you're in the branch of gratitude called Thanksgiving, the bowl of life is overflowing. And you're so grateful that there's another, because all you want to do is give and share and serve and contribute. And that's so fulfilling, it puts you back in the great fullness of life.

So you can live in that cycle. You can actually live in that cycle no matter your financial circumstances. And I say that people who stand in this context of enough, sufficiency that overflows into natural true abundance, are the people who are living a life that really matters. And when people are around them, they feel valued. They feel seen. They feel heard. They feel loved. They feel treated with reverence and respect. And that's the source of our prosperity. That's really the source of it. You know, the word *wealth*, the etymology of it is *well-being*. And each of us has a well of being that is infinite. That's the source of our wealth. That's true wealth.

LOUIE SCHWARTZBERG

LOUIE SCHWARTZBERG: I did a TED Talk about nature and beauty, and when they posted it, it kind of hung there for a while and then, boom, it went viral. I really had no idea it would do that, but I think it resonated with people. I think there's a hunger out there where people want to connect to something that's bigger than themselves. And I think through the portal of nature, it can open your heart and you can develop gratitude for the little things in life. It's so easy to be grateful for a flower, for a bug, for a beautiful day.

OPRAH: *Yes. This is what I've come to know, that nature is our greatest spiritual teacher. I see God as part of nature, and nature as an expression of God. I see it all intertwined. So what has nature taught you?*

LOUIE: Oh, it is God. Because it is personified. And to be able to capture it, and the way I do it with a camera and time lapse and slow motion, I'm able to unveil the mystery of nature and make the invisible visible, unveiling the mysteries of life.

NORMAN LEAR

OPRAH: *You say, if you had one image of God, it would be* thank you *spelled out.*

NORMAN LEAR: Yes. Because of my friend Martin Marty, a great theologian at the University of Chicago for a great many years. I was walking with him in Vermont one day, and I asked him, "Marty, what is the shortest description of worship you can give me?" He said, "One word, Norman."

Gratitude.

Worship is gratitude. It has always felt that way to me.

Everybody has a calling.
Your real job in life is to
figure out why you are
here and get about the
business of doing it.

—*Oprah*

CHAPTER NINE

FULFILLMENT

I created *Super Soul Sunday* in part because of my own yearning to talk to people who have the ability to open both hearts and minds through the wisdom of their life experiences.

Beyond the joy it brings to me, I see the show as an offering to anyone in search of a connection to all that is greater than themselves. Even during *The Oprah Winfrey Show* years, I always felt a hunger from the audience, a deep desire to nourish not only their mind and body but also to create a more meaningful, authentic life.

Most people say the biggest dream they have for themselves is happiness. Contentment and a sense of peace are absolutely elements in the equation, but ultimately, I believe what we're all truly seeking is freedom. We long for a life without constraint, free from conflict, fear, or judgment—where our relationships, career, health, and finances coexist in perfect flow with our spiritual center.

This is what Michael Singer described during our *Super Soul* conversation as an "absolute state of well-being."

As you think about what lasting fulfillment looks like in your own life, know that the divine force at work within all of us has a bigger dream for you than you could ever imagine for yourself. Success comes when you surrender to that dream and allow it to lead you to the next best place.

Outside my office door at Harpo Studios in Chicago, there was an elevator. Every day, I rode it to the studio to tape the show. It was only one floor down, and I could have easily walked, but those precious moments alone were my opportunity to set my intention to bring the very best of myself to both the guests and the audience. I said the same prayer then that I say now before every *Super Soul Sunday* interview:

"Use me, God. Show me how to take who I am, who I want to be, and what I can do, and use me for a purpose greater than myself."

The key to realizing a dream is to focus not on success but on service. Ask yourself, what are the gifts and talents you can share to raise the collective consciousness of all that you encounter? Making that shift from self to service will bring an immeasurable amount of fulfillment to your job, your relationships, and the vision you have of your own best life.

Gary Zukav brilliantly describes this as the moment you discover your authentic power:

"When your personality comes fully to serve the energy of its soul."

Fulfilling your purpose, with meaning, is what gives you that powerful spark of energy unique to only you. The result is an electrifying current of clarity rising from the deepest part of yourself. By tapping into that source, you will no longer feel like the salmon swimming upstream. Instead, people will finally see the highest, truest version of you and stand in awe, wondering how you achieved your dreams.

As you read this chapter, my hope is that you will find the courage to tune out the negative voices telling you all the reasons to give up. Make the choice to turn up the volume to your unique calling, the glory that is your own life.

—*Oprah*

GARY ZUKAV

GARY ZUKAV: The soul is your mother ship. So when you're sailing in the same direction that it wants to go, your life fills with meaning and purpose. And when you sail in another direction, it empties of meaning and purpose. You are a personality. That means you were born on a certain day and you'll die on a certain day. But your soul won't die. Your soul is you also. We're on a journey to the soul, while we're here in this span between birth and death. Think of yourself as a body in a soul.

And while we have this precious opportunity to walk on the earth, the question becomes what will we do with this personality? What will you do with you? Now, here we can define *you* in a couple of ways. One is you with a little *y*. The personality that was born and that will die. The other you is the you with a big *Y*. That's your soul. And if you use your time while you're on the earth to align the little you with the big you, your life begins to fill with meaning, fill with purpose, fill with joy. And you know why you're alive. Following what you know your soul wants you to do.

OPRAH: *One of the things that impressed me the most, it really just stayed with me forever, is when you said, "When the personality comes fully to serve the energy of the soul, that is authentic power." That awakened a spark of knowing in me that I never knew existed. I realized, "Oh, when my personality comes to fully align with the energy of my soul and I allow my soul to be the guide, that is when I am the most powerful. That is when I am in what I now call my sweet spot."*

GARY: You were born to live in the sweet spot. That is the creation of authentic power. And that's how we're all evolving now.

MASTIN KIPP

MASTIN KIPP: I watched Joseph Campbell's *The Power of Myth* film once a year, every year like clockwork. Not because it changed, but because I change. He says that we are not looking for the meaning of life as much as we are looking for the experience of being alive. And, you know, Campbell's coined phrase that sums up his whole life's work of everything he ever studied is "follow your bliss."

OPRAH: *Yes.*

MASTIN: And it's turned into this kind of trite tattoo. But you have to understand, this guy studied all human stories and mythologies and religions and everything, and this is his advice to us: Follow your bliss. So that means pay attention to those moments when you're lit up, when time just flies by. When you're in that field of joyful expression, which is generally in contribution and being in service of some kind. Some sense of connection in your life.

And then to be able to take action in that direction and trust that as you step, something will come to support you. So instead of, *What can I get? How can I take? How can I manipulate?*, the question is, *What can I give?* And when you look at what makes you happy, what makes you come alive, as in following your bliss, you look at those patterns, because if you look back, they're there. And you step out into that.

OPRAH: *What makes you happy? What makes you come alive? What is your bliss?*

MASTIN: You can talk to people. When am I most happy? Ask your friends. Ask your parents.

OPRAH: *I'm most happy in these conversations.*

PAULO COELHO

OPRAH: *One of the running themes throughout* The Alchemist *is one of my favorite all-time quotes. And that is, "When you want something, all the Universe conspires in helping you to get it." I think that's what actually conspired in helping me be here today. I've been trying to do this interview for ten years. But where did that idea, those words, that theme, come from?*

PAULO COELHO: Well, what I experienced in my life is that when I really wanted something, I always got it. Positive and negative. Because the Universe does not think. You have this subconscious mind that sometimes is attracting tragedy. Attracting bad things, you know? Because you want to be a victim. Because to be a victim is to justify a lot of frustrations and failures in your life. The Universe is helping you. You want to be successful. The Universe is helping you.

OPRAH: *Based on how you think, how you truly think, consciously and subconsciously. Do you believe every person has what you call a personal legend?*

PAULO: I'm 100 percent convinced. Which is totally different than I believe that every person is going to fulfill his or her personal legend. All right?

OPRAH: *Okay. I would agree. Every person has a personal legend. First of all, what is a personal legend?*

PAULO: It is the reason that you are here. It's as simple as this. You know? You are here to honor something called the miracle of life. You can be here to fulfill your hours and days with something that is meaningless. But you know that you have a reason to be here. It is the only thing that gives you enthusiasm. And you know when you are betraying your personal legend, when you are doing something without enthusiasm. And, worse, you know that you have this good excuse: I'm not ready. Which is just an excuse. You know? No, I'm not ready. I have to wait for the right moment. You know, now I have to feed my family. Come on. Your family wants to see you happy. Your daughter. Your husband. Your wife. They don't want to see you there sitting in a work that you hate. Even if it gives you tons of money.

OPRAH: *Okay. So you've just given a really key clue to how to know you're pursuing your personal legend. It is that which in life gives you enthusiasm. You call it personal legend. I call it personal calling. Everybody has a reason why you're here. You're called here. And you know if you're on the path to it whether you're enthusiastic about it or not. That's how you know.*

PAULO: One hundred percent. We know our reason to be here. We don't know if we are taking the right steps towards it. But if we are honest enough, God is going to guide you. Even if you take some wrong steps, you know? God will recognize that you have a pure heart. And He puts you back on track.

OPRAH: *Because Life rises up to meet you.*

PAULO: Absolutely.

SUE MONK KIDD

I think we all have something that pulls the soul and that we can give and contribute. Something that lights us up. And when we talk about it, you can often see the lights come on in people.

And we have to stop sometimes. Pause. Hit the Stop button. And really listen to ourselves. Listen to the yearning in ourselves. It's talking to us.

I made this trip to Greece in 1993, and I was on the island of Crete. And we went to this little Greek Orthodox convent, very old. There's a tree there that is sacred to these nuns. And this little nun, about four-eleven, came over, and she was trying to explain to us that there's a tradition that you go up to the tree and you ask for the thing, and she described it like this: In the bottom of your heart. What she was trying to say was ask for the deepest thing in yourself.

But it came out, "Ask for the thing that lies in the bottom of your heart." I never forgot that. And I thought how many women have this thing that lies in the bottom of their heart that they aren't paying attention to that wants to be there. That wants a place in their life.

And so we all took a turn, the women I was traveling with, and we went up under this tree, where there's this amazing icon of Mary, and we asked for the thing in the bottom of our hearts. And I blurted out, "I want to be a novelist." It kind of took me by surprise.

Sometimes it's that simple that you take a moment and you ask yourself, *What's the thing that lies in the bottom of my heart?* And then it … it just comes up. Sometimes it's like that.

Courage is another important component in all of this. The courage to ask that question. What lies at the bottom of my heart? The courage to set that intention. To announce it. To make the annunciation somewhere. Even if it takes our own breath. We should take our own breath once in a while.

Pastor WINTLEY PHIPPS

OPRAH: *You say that God has for all of us a supreme moment of destiny.*

PASTOR WINTLEY PHIPPS: I look at your life and I look at my own life. We have been chasing moments of destiny. You know, the things that you dream of as a kid, and then you watch them come to reality. Those are moments of destiny. But then I began to realize God showed me that moments of destiny are moments for which you were created, but they're not the reason for which you were created. The reason for which we were created is to grow every day to more resemble, reflect, and reveal the character of the one who created us.

OPRAH: *What we're talking about is aligning with that which is the reason why you really came. And that is pursuing whatever is your best destiny. Every person who pursues that with the idea to resemble, reveal, and reflect that which is the character of your creator, you are then on the right path.*

WINTLEY: And whether you are tall or short, whether you are poor or wealthy, you can achieve the destiny for which you were created.

OPRAH: *Ah. Which is what we're all trying to do.*

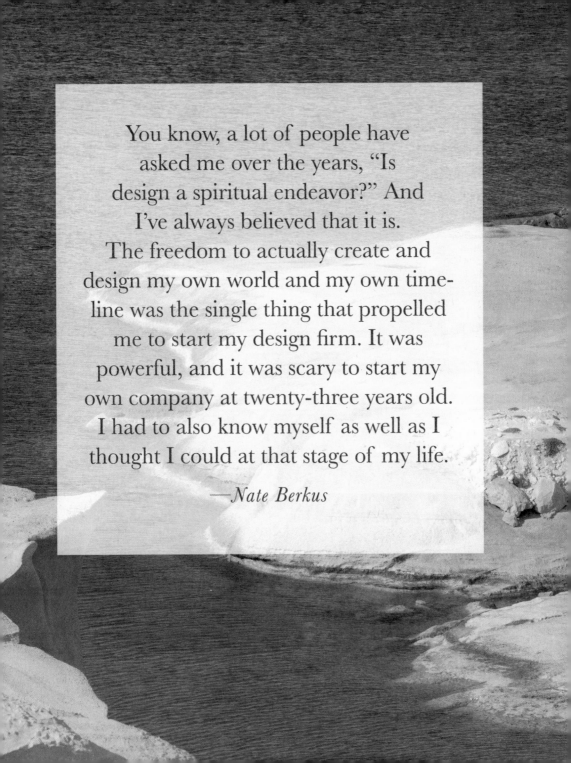

You know, a lot of people have asked me over the years, "Is design a spiritual endeavor?" And I've always believed that it is. The freedom to actually create and design my own world and my own time-line was the single thing that propelled me to start my design firm. It was powerful, and it was scary to start my own company at twenty-three years old. I had to also know myself as well as I thought I could at that stage of my life.

—*Nate Berkus*

The will is so undefinable and can push you so far beyond. I've had sports scientists, the best of them, write me and say, "I'm sorry to tell you, this is humanly impossible." And I write back and say to them, "You have no idea then. You're just doing your little studies on what the heart can do, and what the lungs can do. I'm talking to you about what the spirit can do, and that's not measurable." The spirit is larger than the body. Find a way.

—*Diana Nyad*

INDIA ARIE

The way I visualized it was I had built this big building, and it was pretty from the outside. It was shiny and pretty, and in my mind, it was round like one of those round high-rises. But inside it was just stuff all over the place and people just, you know, running amok. That's how it showed up in my meditation. And when I decided I was going to tear that building down, it was because I had this clarity that ten years from now, I'm going to be in my mid-forties. And I can't have that shiny building on the outside that's a mess inside. It almost makes me want to cry just thinking about it because I didn't know how I was going to do it. I was afraid. I didn't know how to run my business. I was afraid. But I knew that I couldn't keep doing the same thing or I was going to be off the path of my destiny. And that's death. It's not even being alive if you're not doing what you're here to do.

JANET MOCK

OPRAH: *So the reason why this is to me a deeply spiritual conversation is because the search for your authentic self is the search that all of us hold as the pathway on our journey to becoming the highest vision of ourselves. And I think it's so interesting that it took you the time that it took you to become comfortable with telling your story. And when you finally did, for* Marie Claire *in 2011, very few people knew at the time that you were trans. And you kept it quiet because you didn't want to become othered. Othered. And now we're sitting here on* Super Soul Sunday *talking about what that all means. Do you feel that you've now been othered? Or have you transcended that?*

JANET MOCK: I don't know if I've transcended it yet. I still think that for most people the most interesting part about me is my transness. And so for me, there is an othering about that. But I think there's a lot of power in saying that I will proudly and unapologetically embrace that part of my identity for once. The part of my identity that I was taught growing up to be silent about and ashamed of. And so to own that label and to say that

it is mine and I will stand here in that complicatedness of existing as a person, as a trans person, as a trans woman, I think that there is power in that, but there is still an othering attached to any kind of labels that qualify personhood or humanness.

OPRAH: *But I do think we're on the verge of a new way of thinking about sexuality and gender. And not just sexuality and gender. I think this applies to any person who is human, because we get othered in multiple ways throughout our lives. And your desire to redefine realness, I think, is what everybody is looking for, do you agree?*

JANET: I do. We're all searching for truth. I think there's so much that people are telling you about who you are, and that's where the othering comes in. I was constantly, as a young person, navigating society trying to figure out who I was in relation to what people were telling me I should be. And so for me, *Redefining Realness* was about tapping into my most authentic self. *Who am I to me?* For me, realness is about authenticity. It's about searching and seeking truth. It's about being okay in the nuance of the messiness of figuring out who you are when you may not have the answers yet.

OPRAH: *The first time you looked in the mirror after your sex reassignment surgery, you said you felt authenticated and closer to whole for the first time in your life. Was that an overwhelming moment?*

JANET: It was. I was eighteen years old, and I made so many sacrifices and compromises to go get my girl. And I got my girl. I went out in the world and I got her. I liberated her. I went through an underground railroad of resources to get to that place where I could stand in front of that mirror naked for the first time and lay bare in my truth and say, "This is who I am." And I did that on my own. And so to have that at eighteen, that gift, I felt nothing could stop me after that.

JACK CANFIELD

My belief is that the whole purpose of life is to gain mastery—master our emotions, our finances, our relationships, our consciousness—through meditation, things like that. And it's not about the stuff. All the stuff can be taken away. You know? People lose their fortunes. They lose their reputation. Beautiful spouses die or leave you. But who you became in the process can never be taken away. Never. You are mastering through the process of overcoming these obstacles that you face in life.

I believe we all have unlimited possibilities to become pretty much anything we want because I believe you're not given a dream unless you have the capacity to fulfill it. You won't be allowed to have it. Now, you may need to learn new things. You may need to mentor. Get mentored. You may need to team up. But you have the capacity to do anything you can dream up.

We are busier than any other generation we have seen in the last three to four hundred years. We are so busy. And we think because we're busy, we're effective. But I want you to challenge your schedule for a minute and ask yourself, are you really being effective, or is your life cluttered with all kinds of stuff that demands you, and drains you, and taxes you, and stops you from being your highest and best self? And are you substituting busyness and all the chaos that goes along with busyness for being effective?

—*Bishop T. D. Jakes*

DANIEL PINK

DANIEL PINK: We use an exercise with these two parts. The first is you ask yourself, "What is your sentence?" This comes from a famous story about Clare Boothe Luce, who said to President Kennedy, "Hey, a great man is one sentence. You don't have a sentence, you've got a paragraph, and that doesn't work." And, if you really want to be great, Lincoln had one sentence: "He preserved the Union and freed the slaves." Good, good sentence. FDR had a sentence: "He lifted us out of a great depression and helped us win a world war." Awesome sentence. And she went to Kennedy and said, "Listen, a great man is one sentence." A great person is a sentence. And I find that really useful in sort of orienting our lives to our purpose and asking ourselves, "What's your sentence?" And I think that's really clarifying for people.

OPRAH: *Do you know what mine is? I was thinking about this last night. I was thinking,* well what I want it to be is, *"I teach people to lead their best lives by leading my own."*

DANIEL: Whoa. That's a good sentence.

OPRAH: *And what's your sentence?*

DANIEL: Man, I don't want to follow that one. My sentence as I thought about this was, "He wrote books that help people understand the world a little more clearly and live their lives a little more fully."

OPRAH: *Oh, that's good.*

DANIEL: The second question is really important because it helps us get better and move toward mastery day to day. And so the second question to ask yourself at the end of the day, "Was I better today than yesterday?" Because that's really all we can ask for. And what I have found when I ask myself at the end of the day, "Was I better today than yesterday?" is that many times the answer is no. But I find that the answer is rarely no two days in a row. If the answer is no when I go to sleep, I'm just a little ticked off and wake up the next morning with a little bit more resolve. Like, "Oh, great, I wasn't better today than yesterday. That was a waste. Let's not do that again." And that's how we make progress. We do it slowly, step by step by step.

DANIEL GOLEMAN

DANIEL GOLEMAN: I once was giving a talk to a roomful of CEOs, and I said, "How many of you were valedictorians, like, the smartest kid in your class?" Two, three hundred people … three hands went up in the room. It's not related. This is the big myth that the book shatters. It was an eye-opener for me that your IQ, your academic abilities, your cognitive brilliance are not what's going to matter the most. Actually, that's kind of threshold. It gets you in the game. But once you're in the game, it's how you get along with other people. How you handle yourself.

OPRAH: *So your IQ can tell you what you can do, but it can't tell you how to do it.*

DANIEL: That's right.

Intelligence counts for only 25 percent of our job success; 75 percent of our successes in life—and not just about jobs but within the working world—75 percent of what causes our kids to be successful, causes us to be successful, is not about our intelligence and technical skills. It's how we process the world. It's our optimism. Like the belief that our behavior really matters.

—*Shawn Achor*

The least compassionate thing you can do when someone is not equipped to be doing what they're doing is to leave them in that role. They lose confidence and self-esteem. They take that back to their teams. People see that you're leaving them in the role, which undermines your ability to lead. And worst of all, is that individual who no longer believes in themselves, who's losing their sense of self, they're taking that energy home. They're taking that energy home to their families.

—*Jeff Weiner*

WES MOORE

WES MOORE: I'd just come back from Afghanistan and was talking with my mentor, who asked, "What are you planning on doing next with your life?" And I told him I was going to go work on Wall Street. And I expected him to be excited, and he was like, "Really?" And I told him, "That's not the answer that I thought you were going to give me." And he said, "Why are you going to do that?" And I started giving him all these reasons.

OPRAH: *I'm going to help my grandparents.*

WES: My grandparents. You know, I'm helping my family financially. I'm going to be around really smart people. All this kind of stuff. And he said to me, "You know, you just explained to me for the past three minutes why you're doing it, and not once did the words 'because I'm passionate' come out of your mouth." And he said, "Listen, Wes, I'm never going to judge you, and I'm never going to judge the

decisions you make, particularly if you feel like they're in the best interests of your family. The only thing I ask is this: The moment that you feel that you can leave that place, leave. Because every moment you stay longer than you have to, you will become extraordinarily ordinary."

That felt like an indictment. Because I feel like we all spend our time trying to be extraordinary in some way, shape, or form. And the idea that you think you're doing what is the right thing to do and this person is telling you, "But the longer you do it, you will become extraordinarily ordinary." Because if you're not passionate about it, then you'll never be able to fall into your own truth.

OPRAH: *Absolutely. When you were first told about going to Wall Street, though, you said, "In the back of my mind, I heard the rattle of expensive handcuffs."*

WES: Yes. Those things are real. It's like, "Well, now my kids are going to this school," or "I have a second car I have to take care of." Whatever it is. Those things that we're now making decisions based on.

OPRAH: *Yes. "I got here. Now I have to keep doing this. To maintain the life as I now know it."*

WES: That's exactly right.

OPRAH: *Had you been feeling a sense of unease or unhappiness? Were you all the way to unhappy? Or just a sense of* What am I doing?

WES: It was actually, I think, an interesting marriage of both that I was having a difficult time understanding which one was which.

Where I felt like I knew with everything going on that this wasn't where my joy lasted. I knew it was incredibly risky to go out, but I think I had to make a very conscious decision that I would rather flirt with failure than never dance with my joy. Because I felt like I was constantly searching through an occupation to find my joy. And I realized it's not about your occupation, it's about your work. Because they're two different things. My work was where my greatest joy actually started combining with the world's greatest need. And that's when I said to myself, "That's what real service is."

SHONDA RHIMES

When I was a kid, my father used to say to me all the time, "The only limit to your success is your own imagination." And I took that as not just being financial success or work success. I took that as being every kind of success—love and family and emotional and everything. The only limit to your success is your own imagination. Whatever you can imagine is possible.

As a successful woman, a single mother of three, who constantly gets asked the question, "How do you do it all?" the answer is this: I don't. If I am accepting a prestigious award, I am missing my baby's first swim lesson. If I am at my daughter's debut in her school musical, I am missing Sandra Oh's last scene ever being filmed on *Grey's Anatomy*. If I am succeeding at one, I am inevitably failing at the other. That is the trade-off. And yet I want my daughters to see me and know me as a woman who works. I want that example set for them. I like how proud they are when they come to my offices and know that they've come to ShondaLand. There is a land, and it is named after their mother.

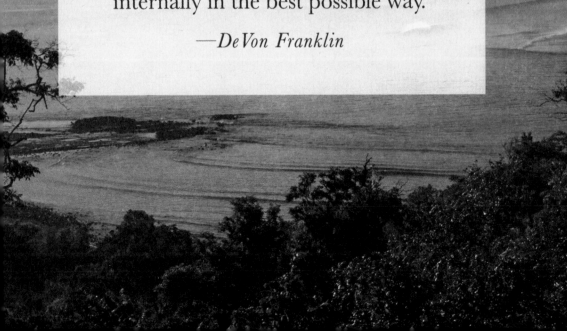

You are fulfilled when you get up in the morning. So many times we get up in the morning, we're depressed. We're down. We're angry. We're frustrated. But when you can wake up saying, "I'm glad to be alive. There is purpose to this day." To me, that is success. And I would argue that once you have that internal success, then externally it's just a manifestation of what happens internally in the best possible way.

—*DeVon Franklin*

I believe three of the most important words anyone can say are not I love you, *but* I hear you.

—*Oprah*

CHAPTER TEN

LOVE AND CONNECTION

At this moment in our history, there is a painful divide separating the human experience.

As I grow more deeply in my spiritual practice, I know the common thread we all share is a mutual desire for connection and contentment. It is up to each one of us to begin the work to renew and repair that bond.

I like to visualize the communication in any relationship as a dance. One person takes a step forward and the other steps back, two energies moving in harmony, aligned and united—until there is a misstep or a break in the connection. If the breakdown is not addressed and corrected in the moment, both people wind up in a tangle of confusion.

When spiritual teacher Adyashanti joined me on *Super Soul Sunday*, he described that "rhythm" we create between one another as the intuitive presence in one soul recognizing the intuitive presence in another. His lesson is that every day, in every moment, our energy is seeking a way to connect with every other energy we encounter. And when we feel that, it means that we have fully aligned, presence to presence, to the Source that exists in us all.

Everything we do, every relationship we have, succeeds or fails based on our level of true spiritual connection.

So how do we get back in step when we find ourselves disconnected and retreating to separate corners of the dance floor? I have learned over the years that the most effective method to find common ground is to approach the person with heartfelt compassion and ask, "What is it that you really want?"

If you allow them the quiet space to respond authentically, most people will often answer with a variation of the same idea: "I want to know that you value me."

By fully embracing the spiritual principle that what we focus on expands, you will discover that giving your full, uninterrupted attention to one person can change the intensity with which that person shines their light on another ... and so on ... and so on ... and so on ...

The power of collective energy was most profoundly explained to me by Harvard brain scientist Dr. Jill Bolte Taylor. After suffering a devastating hemorrhagic stroke, the function of the left hemisphere of Jill's brain was wiped out. The right hemisphere, which focuses only on the present moment, remained intact. With no memory or language recognition, Jill became acutely aware of the energy surrounding her. As doctors, nurses, and visitors entered her hospital room, Jill determined that there were only two types of people in the world: those who bring energy, and those who drain it away.

The request Jill made of every person who came in contact with her throughout her recovery resonated so deeply with me, I posted it in the makeup room where I meet with producers before every show:

Please take responsibility for the energy you bring into this space.

I realized that for every relationship, not only do I have to be accountable for the energy I bring, but I also have to take responsibility for the energy that I allow from others. I understand that strengthening the bond in any situation is impossible if you're not surrounded by energy that lifts you up.

Now, let's expand that idea to the greater good of the world around us. As Holocaust survivor, Nobel Peace Prize winner, and best-selling author Elie Wiesel so beautifully explained to me:

The opposite of love is not hate, but indifference.

Elie often said his favorite Bible verse was from Leviticus: "Thou shalt not stand idly by."

We know humanity is in need of the healing power that comes from love in all its forms. Use your life to serve the world and you will discover the myriad ways the world offers itself to serve you.

Only we hold the power to transform our collective consciousness. As a spirit dwelling in the ever-evolving human experience, I know that I am no better or worse than any other being.

I simply am.
You simply are.
We are connected.

—*Oprah*

Dr. JILL BOLTE TAYLOR

OPRAH: *So was the entire left hemisphere bleeding?*

DR. JILL BOLTE TAYLOR: Mine, yes. It started relatively small deep inside, but it was a hemorrhage, so it got bigger and bigger over the course of the morning.

OPRAH: *And the left hemisphere does what for us?*

JILL: It's our language, it's our ability to think sequentially, to think methodically, to think linearly, to be able to know A plus B equals C. It's our ability to communicate with the external world.

OPRAH: *And the right hemisphere is the big picture?*

JILL: The right hemisphere is the big picture. All the information. It gives us the context of everything. It's our intuition, our witness or observer. It's our ability to experience peace, deep inner peace. So the two hemispheres are very different in their function.

OPRAH: *And the entire left hemisphere went quiet?*

JILL: Yes, it went totally silent.

OPRAH: *Which means you lost your ego.*

JILL: I lost my ego. I was essentially an infant in a woman's body, and I didn't have any of her recollections of her life.

OPRAH: *So what did exist then? You lost the ego. You lost the sense of* I am, *and your sense of context … "I am a PhD at Harvard. I am …"*

JILL: I wasn't any of that anymore.

OPRAH: *But what you had, though, was a sense of oneness and a sense of peace, and a sense of connection to humanity in a way that you never had before, because all of that other stuff had been quieted.*

JILL: Exactly. When I look at people who have had any kind of trauma, I ask, "What have they gained?" What I gained was this incredible knowingness of deep inner peace and excitement of realizing everything was interconnected. And I lost the boundary of my body, so I felt that I was enormous, as big as the Universe, because I no longer defined that this is where I began and this is where I ended.

Nobody but nobody makes it out
here alone. What really matters now
is love. I mean, that condition in
the human spirit that is so profound
it allows us to rise. Strength, love,
courage, love, kindness, love, that
is really what matters. There has
always been evil and there will always
be evil. But there has always been
good, and there is good now.

—*Dr. Maya Angelou*

Sister JOAN CHITTISTER

I was about twelve and we came home and my little parakeet was gone. I was an only child. This may have seemed strange to people, but that little bird was my companion. I didn't go home to playmates, I went home to Billy. Right? And Billy's now missing. My father moved every piece of furniture in that apartment. My mother looked under every chair. The company came, and then family went to bed, okay? But my heart was breaking. And I got into bed and I put my face down in the pillow and I sobbed. I knew I had to be quiet. I couldn't disturb anybody. But I was crying, my little body heaving. And the next thing I knew was I felt somebody on the floor beside me, and then an arm on my back, and I realized it was my mother. And then I felt somebody on the floor on the other side, and I realized it was my father, and they had their arms around me like this, saying, "That's all right, darling. That's all right. We understand. That's all right." And, as I look back over the years, that's when I learned that humanity is about identifying with somebody else's pain, with being there. With somehow or other knowing that you cannot pass on the road because it's not your bird and it's not your child and it's not your pain. Humanity is the ability to hurt for the others. Because that's the only fuel that will stop the injustice. You must know people as people, and you must do what they need in the middle of their pain.

THICH NHAT HANH

The first mantra is, "Darling, I'm here for you." When you love someone, the best thing you can offer him or her is your presence. How can you love if you are not there? You offer him or her your true presence. You are not preoccupied with the past, or the future, your projects. You are for your beloved one. The second mantra is, "Darling, I know you are there, and I am so happy because you are truly there." You recognize the presence of your beloved one as something very precious. And you use your mindfulness to recognize that, embrace your beloved one with mindfulness and she will bloom like a flower. To be loved means to be recognized as existing. And these two mantras can bring happiness right away. The third mantra is what you practice when your beloved one suffers:

"Darling, I know you suffer. That is why I am here for you." Before you do something to help her, to help him, your presence already can bring some relief. And the fourth mantra is a little bit more difficult. You use it when you suffer. If you believe that your suffering has been caused by your beloved one, you suffer so deeply. And you prefer to go to your room and close the door and suffer alone. You want to punish him or her for having made you suffer. The mantra is, "Darling, I suffer. I am trying my best to practice. Please help me." You go to him. You go to her. And practice that. And if you can bring yourself to say that mantra, you suffer less right away.

GARY ZUKAV *and*
LINDA FRANCIS

OPRAH: *Gary, this is your wife, Linda Francis, whom you call your spiritual partner. A spiritual partnership is …*

GARY ZUKAV AND LINDA FRANCIS: A partnership between equals with the purpose of spiritual growth.

OPRAH: *How do we use a spiritual partnership to create authentic power?*

GARY: Creating authentic power is the reason that a spiritual partnership happens. In other words, Linda and I are spiritual partners. I'm committed to my spiritual growth to creating authentic power. Linda is committed to her spiritual growth. I can't create it for her. She can't create it for me. But I can support her, and she can support me. And as you begin to become someone who is … more interested in becoming emotionally aware and taking responsibility for what you create than in blaming other people, you draw other people to you who are doing the same.

LINDA: I've had many attractions in my life where I'm attracted to someone. But I felt that was really from fear-based parts of my personality that wanted to find someone who would complete me.

OPRAH: *Yes, yes. I actually said this to Tom Cruise a long time ago that that line in* Jerry Maguire, *"You complete me," really messed a lot of people up. There wasn't a dry eye in the movie theater, and all the women went, "Oh, she completes him." When in fact no one completes you.*

LINDA: No, there is no way I could've been in a relationship, a spiritual partnership with Gary, had I not done the work that I had done on myself, because I really got it. I created a life where I was the right person and changed myself rather than trying to find someone to complete me, which really changed everything. And I know I would have never met Gary had I not done that work.

OPRAH: *I think that's so powerful. What you just said resonates with me, and I know* it will for many other people. *The reason I'm emphasizing it is so you can really hear it. That instead of looking for the right person, work to make yourself the right person. And the right person will then be drawn to you based upon the work that you've done for yourself. That's what I hear you say.*

LINDA: That's exactly right.

OPRAH: *The definition is so, for me, clear and poignant. A spiritual partnership is a partnership between equals for the purpose of spiritual growth. What do you mean by equals?*

GARY: If you look at the people around you, some of them are stronger. Some of them are weaker. Some of them can draw. Some of them can write. Some of them are wonderful mothers, and others are wonderful carpenters. All of the inequality that you see are all characteristics of a personality. So when you connect with somebody and you feel equal, that is a soul-to-soul connection. Personalities are not equal.

OPRAH: *Got you! Personalities are not equal, souls are?*

GARY: Correct! Equality is understanding that there is nothing and no one in the Universe more important than you. And there is nothing and no one in the Universe less important than you. Now, here's the thing that equality can teach you. If you don't feel equal, you're going to feel either superior or inferior. And both superiority and inferiority are experiences of parts of the personality that originate in fear. It's not possible to enter a spiritual partnership as an equal except soul to soul. If you're not equal, then you're feeling superior or inferior. And if you are feeling one of those, then you know that a frightened part of your personality is active. So when I'm with Linda, for example, or with anyone that I'm a spiritual partner with, I try to use emotional awareness and see, *Am I feeling inferior? Am I trying to please? Am I distorting who I am because I want something from somebody even if it is just their smile? Or am I feeling superior and entitled and I don't care?* You know, do what you want. Here's who I am. But there's no connection. Either one of those is a frightened part of my personality, and I know that I want to challenge it.

MEAGAN GOOD

I grew up in a predominantly white neighborhood. We were one of two black families. So I always had kind of underlying issues with acceptance, and I just wanted someone to say what I already know, which is that you're enough just the way you are. And the only people that have ever said that really have been my mom or my sister. But we're blood. I needed someone else, if they were coming into my life and being a part of my life for the rest of my life, to love me just this way. And so a lot of that healing has come in marriage, for sure. DeVon [Franklin] has been incredibly nurturing in helping remind me of when someone says something bad about him, he lets it roll off his back. I used to cry about it for like a week, and my feelings would be so hurt. And the healing that he's brought in even that area alone, it just reminds me of who God is. Because even if someone else told me that, I couldn't receive it the way that I receive it because of the respect I have for him.

ROB BELL *and*
KRISTEN BELL

ROB BELL: There's nothing more beautiful than an odd, strange word. Especially if it's got meaning and significance attached to it. So I stumbled across the word while studying the writing of Kabbala mystic Isaac Luria, who lived in Jerusalem. The original word is spelled with a *T*. It's T-Z-I-M-T-Z-U-M, and it means to contract or withdraw. This idea of making someone bigger in your life. Creating space for another.

KRISTEN BELL: When you're married, you create space for this other person to thrive while they're doing the same for you. What that does is create space between you that has an energy to it. And we've recognized this energy in our own relationship. We can tell when it's flowing and bringing life. We can tell when something's blocking it.

ROB: It's when you intentionally give yourself to another, not just, *Well, let's see how this afternoon goes.* No. *I'm in this. I'm in this.*

The secret to long marriage is she was the right person. And we decided fairly early in our life to give each other plenty of space. Rosalynn has her own ideas, her own ambitions, her own goals in life, which, in some ways, are different from mine. I let her do her thing. She lets me do my thing. And we try to resolve our inevitable and fairly frequent differences before we go to bed at night.

—*President Jimmy Carter*

Pastor WINTLEY PHIPPS

If you're going to really love somebody, that means you're going to have faith in them. If you're going to love somebody, you're going to have to have the integrity and the goodness.

If you're going to love somebody, you have to learn to be patient with their strengths and with their weaknesses. Love is when you choose to be at your best when the other person is not at their best. Love is when what you want is never important, but what the other person needs and wants is always paramount.

That's what true love is.

BRENÉ BROWN

OPRAH: *Doesn't vulnerability open the door to having greater intimacy?*

BRENÉ BROWN: I think it's the only door.

OPRAH: *Yes. I agree with you. There is no intimacy where there isn't vulnerability.*

BRENÉ: Think about this. We wake up in the morning. We armor up. We go out into the world with this take-no-prisoners attitude. *You're not going to see me. You're not going to hurt me.* We come home and we don't take that armor off. And so then, all of a sudden, you know, when you talk about sex or intimacy, you get in bed, and all of a sudden, it's like two people in big honking armor outfits. It doesn't work.

OPRAH: *I think that being open is what allows you the confidence to know that everybody else has also felt the same thing. That there's no emotion that you can have that somebody else hasn't had.*

BRENÉ: Ever.

OPRAH: *And that is what carried me through thousands of interviews. I know that whatever I'm feeling, there's at least ten other people who are feeling the same thing.*

BRENÉ: Which is vulnerability and courage.

TRACY MORGAN

OPRAH: *I've met so many comedians who feel like they've got to be funny to be valued—that it's all about the joke and it's all about how funny can you be. And they're always thinking about the next joke. So was this a revelation, to realize that you could be so loved?*

TRACY MORGAN: I feel like I tapped into humanity and love. I really feel like I tapped into it. It's like, I tapped into it, and now people just love you. I mean, when I first came out of the hospital, the first time I ever left my house, there were people crying and hugging me, and it was weird to me. But it felt good. People really care. People care. And it's just made me have this new belief in people again. Now when I come out on stage, I get a standing ovation because that's just people, goodwill, being happy. But then you've got a twenty-second grace period. You've got to go to work after that. You can't forget people paid for these tickets. So I go to work. And I know I've tapped into something that no other comedian can really talk about. I've been to the other side, and I came back bearing gifts. And these jokes that I'm giving you all are the gifts.

PHIL JACKSON

It's such a great community that you have when you play the sport, especially if you get to play it at a high level. This is what *esprit de corps*, the word, exactly comes from. That there's a spirit among this connected group of people. And this spirituality is not about religion, of course. It's about the ability to incorporate other beings in your plans, in your system. And my best nature also elevates their nature. And basketball or sports does this. It does this for us as watchers, too, as spectators. We see something that is a remarkable plan. We want to see it over and over again because it brings an elevated spirit to us that this was not just an individual action.

SHAWN ACHOR

While we might have different definitions of happiness, the triggers for happiness are similar worldwide. It's a deep social connection. The breadth and depth and the meaning in our relationships is one of the greatest predictors of long-term levels of happiness we have. Some of the top researchers in positive psychology found that only 10 percent of our long-term levels of happiness are based upon the external world. Ninety percent of our long-term happiness is how the brain processes the world we find ourselves in.

GLORIA STEINEM

GLORIA STEINEM: I was walking through Indian villages with a Gandhian group trying to get a message of "we care about you" to an area where there had been riots. So we were just traveling by foot and being fed by the villagers. Every night, we would sit around a kerosene lamp and the villagers would tell terrible stories of what was happening. But by the end of a few hours, the very fact that they could talk to each other, that they weren't alone in experiencing this, would begin to transform the group. And the Gandhians had told me guidelines to such talking circles, if you want people to listen to you, you have to listen to them. If you want to know how people live, you have to go where they live. Everyone has a story. You have to listen to each other's stories and sit in a circle. And every movement that we care about—the civil rights movement came out of churches in the South, people testifying and telling their stories, and the women's movement started with women sitting in circles and telling their stories. We are communal people. But it took me a while to realize that what I had learned in India had any application in the rest of my life.

OPRAH: *Well, in order for truth to be truth, it applies to all things.*

GLORIA: Oh, that's very good.

OPRAH: *That's what I figured out in all of my interviews. To be truthful, it has to apply to all things.*

GLORIA: Yes, right, right, right.

BRYAN STEVENSON

BRYAN STEVENSON: My clients have taught me that each person is more than the worst thing they've ever done. Because when I meet them, I meet them through some accusation of something horrific and terrible. And what they teach me is that they're more than that crime. They're more than that worst act. And I really have come to believe that if someone tells a lie, they're not just a liar. If someone takes something that doesn't belong to them, they're not just a thief. Even if you kill somebody, you're not just a killer. And what a just and evolved and compassionate society has to do is to figure out the other things you are.

OPRAH: *How have the lives of your clients informed your own humanity?*

BRYAN: It's taught me that mercy is not something we give to people because they deserve it. Compassion is not something we offer to people because they're owed it. It's what we do because it's the way we find mercy for ourselves. You can't get mercy unless you give it. You can't receive compassion unless you give it. And it's made me want to be merciful and compassionate. It's made me want to understand the people who are unhappy with me, who are hostile to me, who sometimes act as if they hate me. I used to get death threats and bomb threats, and it's made me not want to believe that the people behind those threats are just enemies or haters or bigots. It's made me recognize that they're like my clients. They need someone to get past what's created this burden, this fear, this anger, this hostility.

MALALA YOUSAFZAI

OPRAH: *So this is what's interesting, that living your truth nearly cost you your life. You've said if you're afraid, you can't move forward. And so is courage something that you think other people can develop or give to themselves?*

MALALA YOUSAFZAI: There's this fight between courage and fear. And sometimes we choose fear because we want to protect ourselves. But we don't realize that by choosing fear, we put ourselves in a situation that has a really bad impact on us. So if I would have kept silent in Swat Valley and my father would have kept silent and all of us would have kept silent, then there would not have been that moment when change would have come to us in our valley. So it's better to speak out to … to have that moment when you say, "I'm going to do something for my side." And that needs a bit of courage. So our courage was stronger than our fear. And that is what really changed our lives. There was fear; it wasn't that we just totally were fine with what was going on in our society. We were afraid.

OPRAH: *Has this experience made you less afraid?*

MALALA: Yes. Definitely. Before the attack, I used to think, *How would it feel if you were attacked?* And I had these thoughts coming again and again, and I sometimes did think that I would be attacked. Not really expecting, but these thoughts were coming to my mind. But after I was attacked, as I said in my United Nations speech, that they changed nothing in my life except that weakness, fear, and hopelessness died and strength, power, and courage was born. I feel stronger than before.

OPRAH: *Yes. Malala, finish this sentence. I believe …*

MALALA: I believe and I know for sure that if you have strong commitment within your heart, if you have love in your heart, that you want to do something better, the whole world and the whole Universe supports you and your cause. And I had this simple one-word or one-sentence dream that was to see every child going to school. And I spoke out for it, and my father spoke out for it in this small valley in Pakistan, Swat Valley, and the journey started, and now it's going on and getting better and developing each and every day.

Whatever you do in life … remember… think higher, and feel deeper. Life is not a fist. Life is an open hand waiting for some other hand to enter it in friendship. Ultimately, the answers are so simple. Not simplistic, but so simple.

—*Elie Wiesel*

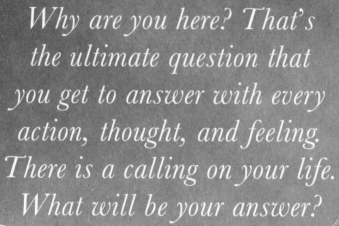

Why are you here? That's the ultimate question that you get to answer with every action, thought, and feeling. There is a calling on your life. What will be your answer?

—*Oprah*

EPILOGUE

In order to experience life, you've got to start asking life's big questions.

With every insight you've experienced from *The Wisdom of Sundays*, you can see that each person on Earth is charting their own spiritual course. Your soul is as unique as your fingerprint. And the journey to connect to the deepest part of yourself can only be explored by you. I've gleaned great understanding from all of these conversations and have come to know that as long as you are asking the right questions of yourself, the answers will readily reveal themselves. Who do you want to be? How can you allow who you want to be to thrive in all aspects of your life?

I often think of this principle when I'm talking with the girls who have graduated from the Oprah Winfrey Leadership Academy in South Africa. I am committed to supporting them through college, and often that simply means being there to listen. This is the time when they start asking, "What should I major in?" or "What do I want to do with my life?" I tell them a career is not a life—the essential question is "Who do you want to be?" And so now I ask you, how can you allow who you want to be to emerge in all aspects of your life?

Most conversations on *Super Soul Sunday* end with a series of "big" questions for each guest. Take the time to ask yourself the same things, and I promise the life vision waiting to be claimed by you will not only unfold, it will expand.

I wish you clarity, love, and, most of all, freedom in your lifelong spiritual adventure.

—Oprah

WHAT IS THE SOUL?

RUSSELL SIMMONS: It is the essential self that is the same in everybody, that isn't defined by personal circumstances and biology. Behind all of that stuff, there is a pure emanating energy that interconnects all beings. That, I think, is the soul.

ELIZABETH LESSER: The soul is like silent music inside. A quiet, beautiful song that you were given to sing here on Earth. God wants you to sing your song. And that's the soul, the song.

DIANA NYAD: A soul is your spirit. It's your love of humanity. It's your belief that there's more than you. There are people before us who you could weep at the thought of, to look at the discovery of an ancient city, and realize that those people lived, and they loved, and they danced, and they

ate, and they suffered, and they lived just as we are. So there have been so many forty- and sixty- and eighty-year lives, billions of them, and we all have souls. I feel their collective souls.

ARIANNA HUFFINGTON: The soul is who I am. The soul is who you are. The body is what allows us to have all these experiences. That means we can evolve through our lives. But who we really are is the soul.

INDIA ARIE: The real you. You do not have a soul. You are a soul. You have a body.

DR. SHEFALI TSABARY: The soul is a mirror of the Universe itself.

MARK NEPO: The soul is the center of Universal Spirit that seeds each human being.

DANIEL PINK: The soul is, I think, our capacity

to see that our lives are about something more than simply the day-to-day and that we're here for a purpose.

DEBBIE FORD: The soul is the part of us that never dies. It's who we are at our core, and it carries all the messages and the lessons that we've learned in the past and will carry all the lessons and the messages into the future.

ECKHART TOLLE: The soul is your innermost being. The presence that you are beyond form. The consciousness that you are beyond form, that is the soul. That is who you are in essence.

LLEWELLYN VAUGHAN-LEE: The soul is the divine part of our self. It is our divine nature. It is the part of us that is one with God. Everybody has a soul. It is the immortal, eternal part of ourselves. It belongs to God.

THOMAS MOORE: The soul loves to be attached. The soul will attach itself. That's why we have soul mates. And we're attached to families and to our kids and to pets and to things, even objects. Even things that we own. We become attached. That's a sign of a real soulful life that you're able to make that attachment.

WHAT IS THE DIFFERENCE BETWEEN SPIRITUALITY AND RELIGION?

ELIZABETH LESSER: Spirituality is this kind of fearless seeking nature. Like, it's the part of us that says, *Whoa. What made a tree? Who am I? Where did I come from? What made something out of nothing? Where do I go when I die? How do I live? How am I supposed to live?* That's spirituality. The seeking of truth. And it takes fearlessness to seek after truth. Religions are our attempt to answer the questions. And some of those answers are great and beautiful. And some of them are just dogma and rules that get us into trouble. "My rules are better than your rules." And then we fight about them. So spirituality is the questioning, and religions are our attempts at answers.

PEMA CHÖDRÖN: Spirituality is like getting into a boat and leaving the shore and going out where you can't see the shoreline anymore. And you're not really sure if you're ever going to get back, because it's big out there. And I guess there would be a lot of different ways people would talk about religion. But nowadays I think we think of it, unfortunately, as that which separates people. Like people holding on to beliefs, where spirituality is about going beyond beliefs. You stop being fixed about how it has to be and who you have to be and it becomes more like a river. You're more like a river than a rock. It keeps moving forward.

IYANLA VANZANT: Religion is the rules, regulation, ceremonies, and rituals developed by man to create conformity and uniformity in the approach to God. Spirituality is God's call in your soul.

SISTER JOAN CHITTISTER: Religion is pointing at the moon. Religion is not the ultimate. Religion is not, itself, the moon, but it is meant to help us see the moon and to require us to reach for it.

DR. MAYA ANGELOU: Religion is like a map. It can help you to see how to get where you want to go. All it does is show you how to get there. It's only a map. Spirituality means surrender. I surrender all to All.

NATE BERKUS: I grew up in a very traditional Jewish culture and religion, but religion wasn't as important as the cultural things around it. For me, defining being more spiritual than religious means that I'm not tied to the religion that I was raised with. I can find my spirituality in anything. And I think I do. I find it in my work and I find it in other people and I find it in teachings from other religions.

SARAH BAN BREATHNACH: Religion says, "There's only one way to heaven." Spirituality says, "Choose the one that brings you joy."

GABRIELLE BERNSTEIN: People find spirituality through religion. But

I think spirituality is an artful craft. We can create our spiritual understanding of our own. We can have a God of our own understanding. We can find God through guitar. We can find God through swimming, through forgiveness. Whatever it is. I think that religion is something we are taught, and spirituality is something we learn and teach ourselves.

WHAT DO YOU THINK IS OUR WORLD'S GREATEST WOUND?

PRESIDENT JIMMY CARTER: The inequity among people. The inability of people who are deprived because of their birth or because of their apparent status to strive for an accomplishment or success and the oppression that is exerted by the powerful and rich people to stay in an ascendant position

in society, economically and culturally.

SHONDA RHIMES: Our inability to realize that we're all the same.

JACK CANFIELD: The greatest wound we've all experienced is somehow being rejected for being our authentic self. And as a result of that, we then try to be what we're not to get approval, love, protection, safety, money, whatever. The real need for all of us is to reconnect with the essence of who we really are and re-own all the disowned parts of ourselves, whether it's our emotions, our spirituality.

WHAT IS THE ROOT OF RACISM?

SHONDA RHIMES: Racism is fear. Everyone is so afraid to have the conversation. I think everyone is so afraid that if they have the conversation, they're either calling someone a racist or they're being called racist or they're going to say the wrong thing. I feel like if you can't have the conversation, you can't make anything change.

SHAKA SENGHOR: The root of racism and prejudice is fear and ignorance. We are so afraid to say, *I don't know. I don't know*, for example, *what it's like to live in that hood.* Or, *I don't know what it's like to live in the suburbs.* And so what we do instead is vilify those things and we create this idea of others.

CHERYL STRAYED: I think the root of racism is in this false notion of the other. Us and them. That kind of divide—that maybe we're not born with, but that we're taught so early on. It's connected to scarcity. It's like we are this tribe and they are that tribe and these people are this. And that idea that

we have to hold power instead of share love.

WHAT DO YOU THINK IS THE PURPOSE OF THIS HUMAN EXPERIENCE? WHY ARE WE HERE?

TIMOTHY SHRIVER: I think we're put here to learn to love unconditionally every fiber and sinew in our bodies and in the Universe. I think we're here for the glory of the idea that we are united. We're not separate. As soon as we get close to that, as soon as we trust that, that's when we realize why we're here.

DR. SHEFALI TSABARY: To reenter that which we left behind. Our wholeness.

LOUIE SCHWARTZBERG: To be connected with the living Universe and realize you're just playing a small part in it.

GRETCHEN RUBIN: I think our purpose is to accept

ourselves and to expect more from ourselves. To understand who we are and to expect ourselves to live up to that ideal better.

MARK NEPO: I think that the purpose of the human experience is for the soul to blossom in human form here on Earth. Rather than finding heaven on earth, I think we are asked to release heaven by living on Earth.

I believe that beyond
this space and time,
all is well and all
will be well.

—*Oprah*

CONTRIBUTORS

SHAWN ACHOR, pp. 165, 190, 215: Shawn Achor is a Harvard University happiness researcher, author, and speaker on the subject of positive psychology. He is the *New York Times* best-selling author of *Before Happiness* and *The Happiness Advantage*. In 2007, Shawn founded GoodThinkInc. and later cofounded The Institute for Applied Positive Research with his wife, Michelle Gielan. Shawn's most recent work is *Unlocking Happiness at Work: How a Data-driven Happiness Strategy Fuels Purpose, Passion, and Performance*, with Jennifer Moss.

ADYASHANTI, pp. 114, 148, 200: Adyashanti is a spiritual teacher and author who offers talks, online study courses, and retreats in the United States and abroad. Together with his wife, Mukti, he is the founder of Open Gate Sangha Inc., a nonprofit organization established in 1996 that supports and makes available his teachings. Adyashanti's best-selling books include *The Way of Liberation, Resurrecting Jesus, Falling into Grace*, and *The End of Your World*. His most recent work is *The Unbelievable Happiness of What Is: Beyond Belief to Love, Fulfillment, and Spiritual Awakening*, with Jon Bernie.

DR. MAYA ANGELOU, pp. 152–153, 203, 223: Maya Angelou was an internationally recognized poet, civil rights activist, and award-winning author known for her acclaimed memoir *I Know Why the Caged Bird Sings* and her numerous poetry and essay collections. Published in 1970, *I Know Why the Caged Bird Sings* made literary history as the first nonfiction best-seller written by an African American woman. Prior to her death in 2014, Maya Angelou had written thirty-six books. She was awarded the Presidential Medal of Freedom in 2010.

INDIA ARIE, pp. 183, 222: India Arie is a four-time Grammy Award-winning singer, songwriter, actress, and musician. She has sold ten million albums worldwide.

REVEREND ED BACON, P. 158: For twenty-one years, Reverend Ed Bacon was the priest and rector at the largest Episcopal congregation in the western United States, All Saints Church, located in Los Angeles. He is a vocal advocate for gay rights and marriage and is the author of *8 Habits of Love: Open Your Heart, Open Your Mind*.

MICHAEL BERNARD BECKWITH, pp. 21, 82–83, 138, 160: Michael Bernard Beckwith is the founder and spiritual director of the Agape International Spiritual Center, a trans-denominational community of thousands. Michael is a sought-after meditation teacher, speaker, and seminar leader whose many books focus on the transformative Life Visioning Process, which he originated. He is the author of several top-selling books, including *Spiritual Liberation and Life Visioning: A Transformative Process for Activating Your Unique Gifts and Highest Potential*.

ROB BELL, pp. 30–31, 209 (*also appears with wife* **KRISTEN BELL, p. 209**)*:* Rob Bell is the *New York Times* best-selling author of *Love Wins, What We Talk About When We Talk About God, The Zimzum of Love* (cowritten with his wife, Kristen), and his most recent book *What is the Bible?* His podcast, the RobCast, is the number one spirituality podcast, and in 2014 Rob was a featured speaker on Oprah's Life You Want Tour. He and Kristen live in Los Angeles with their three kids.

NATE BERKUS, pp. 181, 224:
Nate Berkus first established his
award-winning interior design
firm at the age of 24. Since then,
his approachable and elevated
design philosophy has transformed
countless spaces around the world.
He has produced a number of
successful home collection, and
television shows and is a *New York
Times* best-selling author.

———————

**GABRIELLE BERNSTEIN,
pp. 129, 224:** Gabrielle Bernstein is
an international speaker and author
of the number one *New York Times*
best-seller *The Universe Has Your Back*
and four additional best-selling
books. Gabrielle has been called a
"next-generation thought leader." Her
forthcoming book is *Judgment Detox*.

———————

**SARAH BAN BREATHNACH,
pp. 132–135, 152, 224:** Sarah Ban
Breathnach is a best-selling author,
philanthropist, and public speaker.
She is the author of thirteen books,
including *Simple Abundance: A Daybook
of Comfort and Joy*, which sold over
five million copies and spent more
than two years on the *New York Times*
best-seller list, where it held the
number-one position for a year, and
*Peace and Plenty: Finding Your Path to
Financial Serenity*. Her forthcoming
book is *Starting Over: Discovering the
Spiritual Moxie of Your Swell Dame to
Begin Again*.
www.sarahbanbreathnach.com

DAVID BROOKS, p. 52: David
Brooks is one of the nation's leading
writers and commentators. He is
an op-ed columnist for the *New York
Times* and appears regularly on *PBS
NewsHour* and *Meet the Press*. He is
the best-selling author of *The Road
to Character; The Social Animal: The
Hidden Sources of Love, Character, and
Achievement; Bobos in Paradise: The
New Upper Class and How They Got
There;* and *On Paradise Drive: How
We Live Now (And Always Have) in the
Future Tense.*

———————

**BRENÉ BROWN, pp. 53, 103,
212:** Brené Brown, PhD, is a
research professor at the University
of Houston, where she holds the
Huffington Brené Brown Endowed
Chair at the Graduate College of
Social Work. She has spent the
past fifteen years studying courage,
vulnerability, shame, and empathy
and is the author of three number-
one *New York Times* best-sellers: *The
Gifts of Imperfection, Daring Greatly,*
and *Rising Strong.* Her 2010 TEDx
Houston talk, "The Power of
Vulnerability," is one of the top five
most-viewed TED talks in the world.
For more, visit www.brenebrown.com.

———————

**JACK CANFIELD, pp. 105, 186,
224:** Jack Canfield is the originator
of the beloved *Chicken Soup for the
Soul* series. He has taught millions
his formulas for success, and now
certifies trainers to teach his content

and methodology all over the world.
Jack is the author and coauthor of
more than 150 books, including the
best-selling *The Success Principles:
How to Get From Where You Are to
Where You Want to Be.* He holds the
Guinness World Record for having
the greatest number of books on the
New York Times best-seller list at the
same time.

———————

**PRESIDENT JIMMY CARTER,
pp. 86, 210, 224:** Jimmy Carter
served as the thirty-ninth president
of the United States from 1977
to 1981. In 1982, he became a
University Distinguished Professor
at Emory University in Atlanta,
Georgia, and founded the Carter
Center, which focuses on resolving
conflict, promoting democracy,
protecting human rights, and
preventing disease worldwide.
Jimmy Carter was awarded the
2002 Nobel Peace Prize. He teaches
Sunday school and is a deacon in
the Maranatha Baptist Church of
Plains, Georgia. President Carter
is also the author of twenty-nine
books, including his most recent,
A Full Life: Reflections at Ninety,
published in 2015.

———————

**SISTER JOAN CHITTISTER,
pp. 35, 204, 223:** For forty
years, Sister Joan has passionately
advocated on behalf of peace,
human rights, women's issues, and
church renewal. A Benedictine

sister in Erie, Pennsylvania, Sister Joan is an international lecturer, counselor, and best-selling author of more than fifty books, including her latest, *Radical Spirit*. She writes an online column for National Catholic Reporter and a blog for the Huffington Post. Sister Joan currently serves as cochair of the Global Peace Initiative of Women, a partner organization of the UN.

PEMA CHÖDRÖN, pp. 108, 145, 223: Pema Chödrön is a Buddhist teacher, nun, author, mother, and grandmother. She is widely known for her down-to-earth interpretation of Tibetan Buddhism for Western audiences. She has written several books, including her most recent, *Fail Fail Again Fail Better: Wise Advice for Leaning into the Unknown* and the *New York Times* best-seller *When Things Fall Apart*.

DEEPAK CHOPRA, pp. 20, 68, 147: A world-renowned pioneer in integrative medicine and personal transformation, Deepak Chopra is the founder of the Chopra Foundation, cofounder of Jiyo.com and the Chopra Center for Wellbeing He is the author of more than eighty-five books, including numerous *New York Times* best-sellers. His most recent book is *You Are the Universe: Discovering Your Cosmic Self and Why It Matters.*

PAULO COELHO, p. 178: Paulo Coelho's seminal work *The Alchemist* sold more than 160 million copies worldwide and remained on the *New York Times* best-seller list for 423 weeks. *The Alchemist* is considered one of the most influential spiritual books of all time.

RAM DASS, pp. 27, 156: Ram Dass, one of America's most beloved spiritual figures, has been promoting loving service, harmonious business practices, and conscious care for the dying since 1968. His book *Be Here Now* still stands as the East-meets-West spiritual philosophy on how to live joyously and in the present 100 percent of the time. Ram Dass now resides on Maui, where he shares his teachings through RamDass.org and bi-yearly retreats. His most recent books include *Be Love Now* and *Polishing the Mirror: How to Live from Your Spiritual Heart.*

GLENNON DOYLE, p. 140: Glennon Doyle is the author of the number-one *New York Times* best-seller and Oprah's Book Club selection *Love Warrior*, as well as the *New York Times* best-seller *Carry On, Warrior*. Glennon is a nationally recognized public speaker and the founder of the popular blog Momastery, an online community reaching millions of people each week.

WAYNE DYER, pp. 101, 116: Wayne Dyer, PhD's, first book, *Your Erroneous Zones*, is one of the best-selling books of all time, with an estimated thirty-five million copies sold to date. Over the four decades of his career, he wrote more than forty books, including twenty-one *New York Times* best-sellers. Prior to his death in 2015, Wayne had expanded his message through lecture tours, a series of audiotapes, PBS programs, and regular publication of new books.

DEBBIE FORD, pp. 102, 222: Prior to her death in 2013, Debbie Ford was an internationally recognized expert in the field of personal transformation and a pioneering force in incorporating the study and integration of the human shadow into modern psychological and spiritual practices. She was the *New York Times* best-selling author of nine books, including *The Dark Side of the Light Chasers*, *Spiritual Divorce*, *Why Good People Do Bad Things*, and *The 21-Day Consciousness Cleanse.*

MARIE FORLEO, p. 166: Named by Oprah as a thought leader for the next generation and by *Inc.*'s 500 fastest growing companies for Marie Forleo International, Marie Forleo's mission is to help you build a life you love and use your gifts to change the world. She is the creator of MarieTV, an award-winning online show and podcast that reaches fans in 195 countries. Through her Change Your Life, Change The World initiative, every product purchased helps support a person in need.

DEVON FRANKLIN, pp. 56–57, 197: DeVon Franklin is an award-winning producer, best-selling author, and in-demand preacher and motivational speaker. He also serves as president and CEO of Franklin Entertainment, a dynamic multimedia entertainment company that produces inspirational and commercial content. His most recent projects include the hit film *Miracles From Heaven*; the *New York Times* best-selling book *The Wait*, cowritten with his wife, Meagan Good; and the recently released book *The Hollywood Commandments: A Spiritual Guide to Secular Success*. The excerpt shared in this book contains topics from DeVon Franklin's debut book, *Produced by Faith*.

ELIZABETH GILBERT, pp. 39, 90, 127, 139: Elizabeth Gilbert's 2006 memoir *Eat Pray Love* sparked a global conversation about what it means to fulfill your life's purpose. The book was an international best-seller, translated into over thirty languages, with over ten million copies sold worldwide. Elizabeth has since written several other best-sellers, including her most recent, *Big Magic: Creative Living Beyond Fear*. Elizabeth is a highly sought-after

public speaker, sharing her personal story and insight on personal growth and happiness.

DANIEL GOLEMAN, P. 189: Daniel Goleman is an internationally known psychologist who lectures frequently to professional groups, business audiences, and on college campuses. His groundbreaking book *Emotional Intelligence* was on the *New York Times* best-seller list for a year and a half, with more than five million copies in print worldwide. His most recent work is *A Force for Good*.

MEAGAN GOOD, p. 208: Meagan Good is an award-winning actress and producer. She's also cofounder of the Greater Good Foundation, a nonprofit organization that advocates for the empowerment and enrichment of young women. She's the coauthor of the *New York Times* best-selling book *The Wait*, which she cowrote with her husband, DeVon Franklin.

PASTOR JOHN GRAY, pp. 40–41, 117: John Gray currently serves as an associate pastor at Lakewood Church in Houston, Texas, under the leadership of Pastor Joel Osteen. He is the author of *I Am Number 8: Overlooked and Undervalued, but Not Forgotten by God*. Pastor John and his family are currently starring in the OWN docuseries *The Book of John Gray*.

ARIANNA HUFFINGTON, pp. 66, 222: Arianna Huffington is the founder of the Huffington Post and the founder and CEO of Thrive Global. Her book *Thrive: The Third Metric to Redefining Success and Creating a Life of Well-Being, Wisdom, and Wonder* debuted at number one on the *New York Times* best-seller list. Her most recent work, *The Sleep Revolution: Transforming Your Life, One Night at a Time*, focusing on the science, history, and mystery of sleep, was also an international best-seller.

PHIL JACKSON, p. 214: Legendary NBA coach Phil Jackson was the head coach of the Chicago Bulls from 1989 to 1998, during which Chicago won six NBA championships. His next team, the Los Angeles Lakers, won five championships from 2000 to 2010. Phil says that when he began coaching the Chicago Bulls—and, later, the Los Angeles Lakers—he used the Zen philosophy of mindfulness to help build both teams. In March 2014, Phil was named the president of the New York Knickerbockers—the NBA team he began his professional basketball career with in 1967.

TRACEY JACKSON, 119, 159: Tracey Jackson is an author, blogger, screenwriter, film director, and producer. She has published two books and has written several feature-length screenplays. One of her best-selling books, written with Grammy-winning songwriter Paul Williams, is *Gratitude and Trust: Six Affirmations That Will Change Your Life*. It combines the knowledge Paul gained in his twenty-four years of addiction recovery work with Tracey's lifelong quest for peace and a daily routine to get through life's challenges.

BISHOP T. D. JAKES, p. 187: Bishop T. D. Jakes serves as senior pastor of the Potter's House, a global humanitarian organization and 30,000-member church located in Dallas. His television show, *The Potter's Touch*, reaches sixty-seven million households per month and his best-selling book *Woman Thou Art Loosed* became an award-winning feature film. He is the author of seven *New York Times* best-selling books. His latest work is *Destiny: Step Into Your Purpose*.

JON KABAT-ZINN, p. 64: Jon Kabat-Zinn, PhD, is an internationally known scientist, writer, and meditation teacher. He is a professor of medicine emeritus at the University of Massachusetts Medical School, where he founded its world-renowned Mindfulness-Based Stress Reduction clinic and the Center for Mindfulness in Medicine, Health Care, and Society. Jon is the author of several books, including the best-selling *Full*

Catastrophe Living: Using the Wisdom of Your Body and Mind to Face Stress, Pain, and Illness and *Wherever You Go, There You Are: Mindfulness Meditation in Everyday Life*.

SUE MONK KIDD, pp. 19, 54, 93, 179: When Sue Monk Kidd's first novel, *The Secret Life of Bees*, was published by Viking in 2002, it spent more than two and a half years on the *New York Times* best-seller list and later became a feature film. *The Invention of Wings* was published in 2014, debuted on the *New York Times* best-seller list at number one, and was chosen for Oprah's Book Club 2.0.

MASTIN KIPP, pp. 89, 177: Mastin Kipp is the number one best-selling author of *Daily Love: Growing into Grace* and has been recognized by Oprah Winfrey on her Emmy-winning show *Super Soul Sunday* as a "spiritual thinker for the next generation." Mastin appears alongside Tony Robbins, Eckhart Tolle, Deepak Chopra, Brené Brown, and others as a part of Oprah's Super Soul 100, a collection of awakened leaders who are using their voices and talent to elevate humanity. Mastin leads sold-out seminars and retreats all over the world, and collectively two million people in more than one hundred countries have been influenced by his work.

JACK KORNFIELD, pp. 22–24: Jack Kornfield trained as a Buddhist monk in the monasteries of Thailand, India, and Burma. He has taught meditation internationally since 1974 and is one of the key teachers to introduce Buddhist mindfulness practice to the West. Jack has authored fifteen books, including *No Time Like the Present*.

ANNE LAMOTT, p. 74: Anne Lamott is both a novelist and a nonfiction writer. She is the author of the *New York Times* best-sellers *Small Victories; Stitches; Help, Thanks; Wow; Some Assembly Required; Grace (Eventually); Plan B;* and *Traveling Mercies*. A past recipient of a Guggenheim Fellowship, Anne's most recent work is *Hallelujah Anyway*.

NORMAN LEAR, pp. 71, 171: Norman Lear is a writer, producer, director, and creator of legendary television shows like *All in the Family, Good Times, Sanford and Son, The Jeffersons, Maude,* and many others. He is the founder of both People for the American Way, a nonprofit organization that monitors violations of constitutional freedoms, as well as the Norman Lear Center at the USC Annenberg School for Communication. In October 2014, Norman published his memoir, *Even This I Get to Experience*.

ELIZABETH LESSER, pp. 29, 128, 157, 222, 223: Elizabeth Lesser is cofounder and senior adviser of Omega Institute, the largest adult education center in the United States focusing on health, wellness, spirituality, and creativity. Elizabeth is also the author of the *New York Times* best-selling book *Broken Open: How Difficult Times Can Help Us Grow.* Her latest work, *Marrow: A Love Story,* is a memoir about Elizabeth and her younger sister Maggie's spiritual journey after Elizabeth became the donor for Maggie's bone marrow transplant.

ALI MACGRAW, p. 131: Ali MacGraw is an actress, model, author, spiritual seeker, and animal rights activist. She reached international fame in 1970's *Love Story,* for which she was nominated for an Academy Award for best actress and won the Golden Globe Award for best actress. She went on to star in the popular action films *The Getaway* (1972) and *Convoy* (1978) among others. In 1991, she published an autobiography, *Moving Pictures.*

JANET MOCK, p. 184–185: Janet Mock is a writer, TV host, and advocate whose memoir, *Redefining Realness,* debuted on the *New York Times* best-seller list in 2014. She is a sought-after speaker who gave a rousing speech at the Women's March in Washington and a multi-platform storyteller who produced HBO's *The Trans List.* Janet's latest book is *Surpassing Certainty: What My Twenties Taught Me.*

THOMAS MOORE, pp. 36–37, 223: Thomas Moore is the author of the best-selling book *Care of the Soul* and fifteen other books on deepening spirituality and cultivating the soul. He has been a monk, a musician, a university professor, and a psychotherapist, and today he lectures widely on holistic medicine, spirituality, psychotherapy, and the arts. He has a PhD in religion from Syracuse University and contributes regularly to the blog Patheos.com. His most recent book is *Ageless Soul: Living a Full Life with Joy and Purpose.*

WES MOORE, p. 194–195: Wes Moore is a Rhodes scholar, Army combat veteran, entrepreneur, and author of two *New York Times* best-selling books: *The Other Wes Moore* and *The Work.* He founded BridgeEdU with the hope of offering young scholars a better opportunity to succeed by reinventing the first-year college experience and building a better on-ramp to higher education and career preparedness.

TRACY MORGAN, p. 213: Tracy Morgan is an actor and comedian best known for his eight seasons as a cast member on *Saturday Night Live* and for his costarring role on the Emmy-winning television show *30 Rock.* After surviving a devastating car accident in 2014 that left him in a coma, Tracy says he's "been to the other side" and is forever changed because of it.

CAROLINE MYSS, pp. 14, 15, 84, 136, 163: Caroline is a five-time *New York Times* best-selling author and internationally renowned speaker in the fields of human consciousness, spirituality and mysticism, health, energy medicine, and the science of medical intuition. Her seminal book, *Anatomy of the Spirit,* has sold over 1.5 million copies. Her most recent work is *Archetypes: Who Are You?*

MARK NEPO, pp. 115, 154, 222, 225: Mark Nepo is a poet and philosopher who has taught for more than forty years in the fields of poetry, spirituality, and the journey of inner transformation, and the life of relationships. Mark is best known for his number-one *New York Times* best-seller *The Book of Awakening.* His most recent books are *The One Life We're Given, The Way Under the Way,* and *Things That Join the Sea and the Sky: Field Notes on Living.*

THICH NHAT HANH,
pp. 77, 205: Zen master Thich
Nhat Hanh is a global spiritual
leader, poet, and peace activist,
revered throughout the world for his
powerful teachings and best-selling
writings on mindfulness and peace.
He has founded eleven monasteries
in America, Europe, and Asia, as
well as over one thousand local
mindfulness practice communities,
known as sanghas. He has
published over one hundred titles
on meditation, mindfulness, and
engaged Buddhism, including *Being
Peace, Peace Is Every Step, The Miracle
of Mindfulness*, and his most recent,
*At Home in the World: Stories and
Essential Teachings from a Monk's Life.*

DIANA NYAD, pp. 59, 182, 222:
On September 2, 2013, at the age
of sixty-four, Diana Nyad became
the first person to swim from Cuba
to Florida without the aid of a shark
cage, swimming nonstop 111 miles
in fifty-three hours from Havana to
Key West. In the 1970s, she set the
record for both men and women for
circling Manhattan Island, along
with other open-water records, and
then spent the next thirty years as
a prominent sports broadcaster,
filing for such news entities as
National Public Radio. Diana is the
author of four books, including her
recent memoir, *Find a Way*. With
her Cuba Swim expedition leader,
Bonnie Stoll, Diana has launched
the biggest walking initiative in
American history, EverWalk.com.

JOEL OSTEEN, p. 49: Joel
Osteen is the senior pastor of
America's largest congregation,
Lakewood Church in Houston,
Texas. His televised messages are
seen by more than ten million
viewers each week in the United
States, and millions more in one
hundred nations around the world.
His twenty-four-hour channel
on SiriusXM Satellite Radio
and millions of social media
followers have prompted numerous
publications to name him as one
of the most influential Christian
leaders in the world. He is also
the author of eight *New York Times*
best-sellers, including his two most
recent works: *The Power of I Am* and
*Think Better, Live Better: A Victorious Life
Begins in Your Mind.*

PASTOR WINTLEY PHIPPS,
p. 180, 211: World-renowned
vocal artist Wintley Phipps is also
a pastor, motivational speaker,
and author of *Your Best Destiny:
Becoming the Person You Were Created
to Be*. He is the founder, president,
and chief executive officer of the
US Dream Academy, a national
after-school program that aims to
break the cycle of intergenerational
incarceration by giving children the
skills and vision necessary to lead
productive and fulfilling lives.

DANIEL PINK, pp. 188, 222:
Daniel Pink is the author of five
books about business, work, and

behavior, including three *New York
Times* best-sellers: *A Whole New Mind,
Drive*, and *To Sell Is Human*. His
articles and essays have appeared in
the *New York Times, Harvard Business
Review, The New Republic, Slate*, and
other publications. Daniel's TED
Talk on the science of motivation is
one of the ten most-watched TED
Talks of all time, with more than
nineteen million views.

AMY PURDY, p. 58: Amy Purdy
is one of the top-ranked female
adaptive snowboarders in the
world, a three-time World Cup para
snowboard gold medalist, the 2014
Paralympic bronze medalist, and the
founder of Adaptive Action Sports,
a nonprofit organization that helps
youth, young adults, and wounded
veterans with physical disabilities
get involved with action sports. Amy
was the breakout star and a finalist
on season 18 of *Dancing with the Stars*.
Her memoir, *On My Own Two Feet*,
was published in 2014 and became a
New York Times best-seller.

**SHONDA RHIMES, pp. 65,
196, 224:** Shonda Rhimes is the
critically acclaimed, Emmy-winning
creator and executive producer
of the hit television series *Grey's
Anatomy, Private Practice*, and *Scandal*
and is the executive producer of
How to Get Away with Murder and *The
Catch*. Shonda is also founder of her
production company, Shondaland,
located in Los Angeles, where she

lives with her three daughters. She is the author of *New York Times* best-selling *Year of Yes* and *The Year of Yes Journal.*

TONY ROBBINS, pp. 50, 155: Tony Robbins is a best-selling author, entrepreneur, and philanthropist. For more than four decades, millions of people have enjoyed the warmth, humor, and transformational power of his business and personal development events. He is the nation's number one life and business strategist. He's called upon to coach some of the world's finest athletes, entertainers, CEOs, and leaders of nations. Through his partnership with Feeding America, Tony has provided over 200 million meals in the last two years to those in need. He is on track to provide a billion meals by 2025. He lives in Palm Beach, Florida, with his wife, Sage Robbins.

FATHER RICHARD ROHR, pp. 69, 130: Richard Rohr is a globally recognized ecumenical teacher and founder of the Center for Action and Contemplation in Albuquerque, New Mexico. Richard's teaching is grounded in the practices of contemplation and self-emptying, expressing itself in radical compassion, particularly for the socially marginalized. Richard is also the author of numerous books, including his most recent, *The Divine Dance: The Trinity and Your Transformation.*

GENEEN ROTH, p. 161: Geneen is a highly sought-after public speaker and author of nine books, including *Lost and Found, When Food Is Love,* and the number-one *New York Times* best-seller *Women Food and God.* Her pioneering works were among the first to link compulsive eating and perpetual dieting with deeply personal and spiritual issues that go far beyond food, weight, and body image.

GRETCHEN RUBIN, pp. 164, 225: Gretchen Rubin is the well-known author of several books, including the *New York Times* best-sellers *Better Than Before, The Happiness Project, Happier at Home,* and her most recent book, *The Four Tendencies.* She also has a popular blog and an award-winning podcast, Happier with Gretchen Rubin.

DON MIGUEL RUIZ, p. 118: Don Miguel Ruiz is a spiritual teacher and international best-selling author. His landmark best-selling book, *The Four Agreements,* has sold over 6.5 million copies in the United States and has been translated into forty languages worldwide. It appeared on the *New York Times* best-seller list for over a decade, and 2017 marks the twentieth anniversary of its original publication. His latest works include *The Mastery of Self: A Toltec Guide to Personal Freedom* and *The Toltec Art of Life and Death: Living Your Life as a Work of Art.*

ZAINAB SALBI, p. 76: Zainab Salbi is a humanitarian, author, and media personality who has dedicated herself to women's rights and freedom. At the age of twenty-three, Zainab founded Women for Women International, a grassroots humanitarian and development organization dedicated to serving women survivors of wars. Zainab is the author of several books, including the national best-seller *Between Two Worlds: Escape from Tyranny: Growing Up in the Shadow of Saddam.* She is the creator and host of *The Nida'a Show* and is the editor at large at Women in the World in association with the *New York Times.*

LOUIE SCHWARTZBERG, pp. 170, 225: Louie Schwartzberg is an award-winning cinematographer, director, and producer whose career spans more than four decades. Using breathtaking imagery through time-lapse, high-speed, and macro cinematography techniques, Louie tells stories that celebrate life and reveal the mysteries and wisdom of nature, people, and places. His films include *Wings of Life,* for DisneyNature, and *3D Mysteries of the Unseen World,* for National Geographic.

SHAKA SENGHOR, pp. 120, 225: While serving a nineteen-year sentence for second-degree murder, Shaka Senghor says literature, meditation, self-examination, and the kindness of others helped him find redemption. He was able to forgive those who hurt him and began atoning for the wrongs he committed. Shaka's *New York Times* best-selling memoir, *Writing My Wrongs: Life, Death, and Redemption in an American Prison,* has inspired thousands, and his work to change the narrative around prisons and mass incarceration has earned him numerous awards and fellowships.

TIMOTHY SHRIVER, pp. 94, 225: Timothy P. Shriver, PhD, is a social leader, an educator, and an author. He is the chairman of Special Olympics, and in that capacity, serves over 5.3 million Special Olympic athletes and Unified partners in 169 countries. In 2014, Timothy wrote *Fully Alive: Discovering What Matters Most,* where he shares the life-changing impact of people with intellectual disabilities and their capacity to inspire others to find out about what matters most.

RUSSELL SIMMONS, pp. 67, 167, 222: Russell Simmons is the chairman and CEO of Rush Communications, the co-founder of hip-hop music label Def Jam Recordings, and creator of the clothing fashion lines Phat Farm, Baby Phat, Run Athletics, Argyleculture, and Tantris. He is the author of the *New York Times* best-sellers *Success Through Stillness, Super*

Rich, and *Do You!* His latest book is *The Happy Vegan.*

MICHAEL SINGER, pp. 42–43, 73, 122, 141, 174: Michael Singer is the author of the number one *New York Times* best-seller *The Untethered Soul.* In 1975, he founded Temple of the Universe, a yoga and meditationcenter. Michael is also the creator of a leading-edge software package that transformed the medical practice management industry. His latest book is *The Surrender Experiment: My Journey into Life's Perfection.*

GLORIA STEINEM, p. 216: Gloria Steinem is a writer, lecturer, political activist, and feminist organizer. She travels the world speaking on issues of gender equality. She is cofounder of *New York* magazine, founder of *Ms.* magazine, and among the founders of the National Women's Political Caucus. Most recently, she participated in and spoke at the Women's March in Washington, D.C. Gloria's latest book is her travelogue *My Life on the Road.*

BRYAN STEVENSON, pp. 121, 217: Bryan Stevenson is a lawyer, social justice activist, speaker, founder and executive director of the Equal Justice Initiative, and a clinical professor at New York

University School of Law. He wrote the critically acclaimed book, *Just Mercy: A Story of Justice and Redemption,* published in 2014. It was selected by *Time* magazine as one of the "10 Best Books of Nonfiction" for 2014.

CHERYL STRAYED, pp. 85, 146, 162, 225: Cheryl Strayed is the author of the number one *New York Times* best-seller and Oprah Book Club selection *Wild,* which became a top-selling feature film and garnered Reese Witherspoon an Oscar nomination for her starring role in the adaptation. Cheryl is also the author of the *New York Times* best-sellers *Tiny Beautiful Things* and *Brave Enough,* and the novel *Torch.* She's the cohost of the popular advice podcast, Dear Sugar Radio. Her essays have been published in *The Best American Essays,* the *New York Times,* the *Washington Post Magazine,* and *Vogue,* among others.

DR. JILL BOLTE TAYLOR, pp. 75, 201, 202: Dr. Jill Bolte Taylor is a Harvard-trained neuroanatomist. Her nonprofit organization, JBT Brains, is dedicated to providing educational services and promoting programs related to the advancement of brain awareness. She is the national spokesperson for the Harvard Brain Tissue Resource Center and an active member of the National

Alliance on Mental Illness. Jill is also the author of the *New York Times* best-selling memoir *My Stroke of Insight: A Brain Scientist's Personal Journey.*

ECKHART TOLLE, pp. 18, 98–99, 100, 222: Eckhart Tolle is a spiritual teacher and author who was born in Germany and educated at the Universities of London and Cambridge. He is the author of the number one *New York Times* best-seller *The Power of Now* and the highly acclaimed follow-up *A New Earth,* which are widely regarded as two of the most influential spiritual books of our time.

DR. SHEFALI TSABARY, pp. 104, 144, 222, 225: Dr. Shefali Tsabary is a *New York Times* best-selling author of *The Conscious Parent* and *The Awakened Family,* both hailed by Oprah as the most profound books on parenting she has ever read. Shefali is a clinical psychologist who helps transform her clients using a blend of Eastern mindfulness and Western psychology. Her life's mission is to revolutionize the way we raise our children and thereby help heal the planet.

LYNNE TWIST, p. 168–169: For more than forty years, Lynne Twist has been a recognized global visionary committed to alleviating

poverty, ending world hunger, and supporting social justice and environmental sustainability. Her acclaimed book *The Soul of Money: Transforming Your Relationship with Money and Life* was re-released in April 2017.

IYANLA VANZANT, pp. 51, 72, 113, 142–143, 223: From welfare mother to *New York Times* best-selling author, from the Brooklyn projects to NAACP Image Award winner, from broken pieces to peace, Iyanla Vanzant is one of the country's most prolific writers and public speakers and among the most influential, socially engaged, and acclaimed spiritual life coaches. Executive producer and host of *Iyanla: Fix My Life* on OWN, Iyanla's focus on faith, empowerment, and loving relationships has inspired millions around the world. The author of nineteen books, including an astounding six *New York Times* best-sellers, Iyanla's work has been translated into more than twenty-three languages. Iyanla's no-nonsense approach and underlying message of "live better by loving yourself" has ignited the spark of self-discovery.

LLEWELLYN VAUGHAN-LEE, pp. 32–33, 137, 222: Llewellyn Vaughan-Lee, PhD, is a Sufi teacher and author. In recent years the focus of his writing and teaching has been

on spiritual responsibility in our present time of global crisis, and an awakening global consciousness of oneness. He has written about the feminine, and the emerging subject of spiritual ecology. His latest book is *Spiritual Ecology: 10 Practices to Reawaken the Sacred in Everyday Life.*

JEFF WEINER, pp. 106–107, 193: Jeff Weiner is the CEO of LinkedIn, the world's largest and most powerful network of professionals. Jeff joined the company in December 2008; under his leadership, LinkedIn has rapidly expanded its global platform to twenty-four languages and more than thirty offices around the world, and grown its membership base to more than 467 million members. In addition to LinkedIn, Jeff serves on the board of directors for Intuit Inc. and DonorsChoose.org. He holds a BS in economics from the Wharton School at the University of Pennsylvania.

ELIE WIESEL, pp. 201, 219: Born in Romania, Elie Wiesel was fifteen when he was sent to the Auschwitz concentration camp in Poland with his family in 1944. He was later moved to and ultimately freed from the Buchenwald camp in 1945. Of his relatives, only two of his sisters survived. Prior to his death in 2016, Elie established the Elie Wiesel Foundation for Humanity with his wife, Marion Wiesel, and authored more than sixty books of fiction and nonfiction. For his literary and human rights efforts, he received prestigious awards, including the Nobel Prize for Peace, the Presidential Medal of Freedom, the US Congressional Gold Medal, and the National Humanities Medal.

PAUL WILLIAMS, p. 159: Paul Williams is a five-time Grammy-winning composer, singer, and songwriter. He received his certification from UCLA as a drug rehabilitation counselor and shares lessons and his own journey to recovery in *Gratitude and Trust: Recovery Is Not Just for Addicts,* co-written with Tracey Jackson. Tracey and Paul also host the Gratitude and Trust Podcast.

MARIANNE WILLIAMSON, p. 91: Marianne Williamson is an internationally acclaimed spiritual writer and lecturer. She is the author of twelve books, seven of which were *New York Times* best-sellers. Her work *A Return to Love* is considered one of the most influential in spirituality today. In 1989, Marianne founded Project Angel Food, a meals-on-wheels program that serves homebound people with AIDS in the Los Angeles area. To date, Project Angel Food has served over ten million meals. Marianne's most recent book, *Tears to Triumph,* was published in 2016.

RAINN WILSON, p. 70: Rainn Wilson is an actor, writer, and cocreator of media and production company SoulPancake. Best known for playing Dwight Schrute on NBC's Emmy-winning *The Office,* Rainn is a board member of Mona Foundation and co-founded Lidè, an educational initiative in rural Haiti that empowers young, at-risk women through the arts. He is the author of *Bassoon King.*

MALALA YOUSAFZAI, P. 218: In 2012, when she was fifteen, Malala Yousafzai became an international symbol of hope after she was shot in the head at point-blank range while riding the bus home from school. Since then, Malala has become an activist for female education and the youngest-ever Nobel Prize laureate. Her book *I Am Malala* became an international best-seller.

GARY ZUKAV, pp. 16, 46, 48, 175, 176, 206-207 (*also appears with his spiritual partner,* **LINDA FRANCIS, 206-207**): A master spiritual teacher and author of four consecutive *New York Times* best-sellers, Gary Zukav and his seminal book *Seat of the Soul* led the way to seeing the alignment of the personality and the soul as the fulfillment of life and captured the imagination of millions. It was a number one *New York Times* best-seller thirty-one times and remained

on the *New York Times* best-seller list for three years. Gary and his wife and spiritual partner, Linda Francis, cofounded the Seat of the Soul Institute, dedicated to assisting people across the world in the creation of authentic power.

ABOUT THE AUTHOR

———————————

OVER THE COURSE of her esteemed career, Oprah Winfrey has created an unparalleled connection with people around the world. As host and supervising producer of the top-rated, award-winning *The Oprah Winfrey Show*, she entertained, enlightened, and uplifted millions of viewers for twenty-five years.

Her accomplishments as a global media leader and philanthropist have established her as one of the most influential and admired public figures in the world today.

CREDITS *and* ACKNOWLEDGMENTS

This book was produced by

 MELCHER MEDIA

124 West 13th Street
New York, NY 10011
www.melcher.com

President and CEO: Charles Melcher
Vice President and COO: Bonnie Eldon
Executive Editor/Producer: Lauren Nathan
Senior Editor/Producer: Aaron Kenedi
Production Director: Susan Lynch
Senior Digital Producer: Shannon Fanuko
Associate Editor/Producer: Victoria Spencer

MELCHER MEDIA WOULD LIKE TO THANK:

Callie Barlow, Jess Bass, Trina Bentley, Emma Blackwood, Renee Bollier, Melissa Gidney Daly, Karl Daum, Ashley Gould, Heather L. Hughes, Erica Jago, Luke Jarvis, Emma McIntosh, Karolina Manko, Lauren McGlade, Josh Raab, Rachel Schlotfeldt, Megan Worman, Katy Yudin, and Gabe Zetter.

THANK YOU TO:

Oprah Winfrey Network and Discovery Communications, Inc.

ARTWORK CREDIT:

Page 47: *Grupo de cuatro mujeres de pie* by Francisco Zúñiga © Fundación Zúñiga Laborde A.C. (Mexico)